I0759578

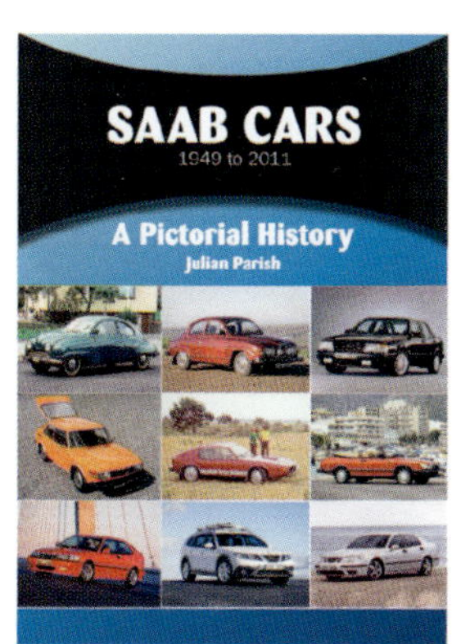
SAAB CARS
1949 to 2011
A Pictorial History
Julian Parish

A Pictorial History – **more titles in this series**

Austin Cars 1948 to 1990 (Rowe)
Bentley Cars 1933 to 2020 (Taylor)
BMW Cars 1945 to 2113 (Alder)
Citroën Cars 1934 to 1986 (Parish)
Ford Cars – Ford UK cars 1945-1995 (Rowe)
Jaguar Cars 1946 to 2008 (Thorley)
Lotus Cars 1952 to 2024 (Vale)
Mercedes Benz Cars 1947 to 2000 (Taylor)
MG Cars 1930 to 2006 (Alder)
Morris Cars 1948 to 1984 (Newell)
Riley & Wolseley Cars 1948 to 1975 (Rowe)
Rootes Cars of the 50s, 60s & 70s (Hillman, Humber, Singer, Sunbeam & Talbot) (Rowe)
Rover Cars 1945 to 2005 (Taylor)
Triumph & Standard Cars 1945 to 1984 (Warrington)
Vauxhall Cars 1945 to 1995 (Alder)
Volvo Cars 1945 to 1995 (Alder)

www.veloce.co.uk

First published in 2025 by Veloce, an imprint of David and Charles Limited. Tel +44 (0)1305 260068 / e-mail info@veloce.co.uk web www.veloce.co.uk.
ISBN: 9781836440321 Readers with ideas for automotive books, or books on other transport or related hobby subjects, are invited to write to the editorial director of Veloce at the above address. British Library Cataloguing in Publication Data – A catalogue record for this book is available from the British Library. Design and production by Veloce. Printed and bound in the UK by Short Run Press Ltd.

SAAB CARS

1949 to 2011

A Pictorial History

Julian Parish

CONTENTS

INTRODUCTION

Nearly 15 years after the last cars rolled off the production lines in Trollhättan, Saab still commands a keen following among car enthusiasts around the world. Beginning with the first 92 in 1949, Saab became renowned for the aerodynamic design, technical innovation, and sturdy construction of its cars; they famously appealed to individualists and creative thinkers, who were fiercely loyal to the brand.

Like its Swedish counterpart Volvo, Saab always set great store by safety – both active and passive – and respect for the environment. From the very beginning, however, its cars also became an enthusiast's choice, with dynamic handling and a level of performance that belied their modest engines. The company's many successes in rallying, thanks to drivers like the great Erik Carlsson, and its pioneering use of turbocharging cemented its sporting reputation.

For more than 60 years as a car maker, Saab traded strongly on its origins in aviation, a story that began shortly before the Second World War. In 1936, the Swedish government decided to increase its spending on defence and to create a Swedish Air Force. In April the following year, a new consortium, the Svenska Aeroplan Aktiebolaget (the Swedish Aeroplane Corporation, soon known simply by the acronym SAAB) was formally established. It began building planes under licence from Junkers and Northrop in 1938, followed in March 1940 by the first Saab-branded plane, the Saab 17 dive-bomber.

As the war came to an end in 1945 and demand for military aircraft slowed, Saab's management realised that the company needed to diversify. It therefore set up a team of 15 staff led by the aeronautical engineer Gunnar Ljungström to develop an all-new car. None of them had any prior experience in the car industry, but their knowledge of engineering and aerodynamics was soon put to good use.

On 10 June 1947, the very first Saab car – the so-called 'Ursaab' – was revealed to the world's press in the homely surroundings of the company's staff canteen at Linköping. Over the next two years, the initial prototype was further developed and prepared for production as the Saab 92. It was an aerodynamically styled two-door saloon, powered by a two-cylinder, two-stroke engine. Like nearly all the Saabs that followed, it had front-wheel drive.

At the end of 1955, the 92 made way for the 93. Like the original model, it was available only as a two-door saloon, but with more flowing lines and an Italian-inspired frontal treatment. Above all, it had a completely new three-cylinder engine. The 93's mechanicals were the basis for the first Sonett, a two-seat roadster also known officially as the Saab 94. This was presented in 1956 but never went into full-scale production.

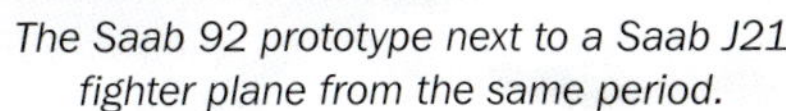

The Saab 92 prototype next to a Saab J21 fighter plane from the same period.

One of Rony Lutz' famous drawings for Saab; this one is a 1956 93A.

Saab's production grew steadily through the 1950s, with sales to export markets, and to the US in particular, becoming increasingly important. In 1959, Saab introduced its first-ever estate car, the three-door 95, with seating for up to seven passengers. Initially powered by the same three-cylinder engine as the 93, it later received a 1.5-litre four-stroke V4 supplied by Ford.

The 96 saloon was launched soon after the 95, at the start of 1960, with a similar specification to the estate. It was the first Saab officially sold in the UK. Like the 93, the 96 also served as the basis for a sports car, the Sonett II (or type 97) coupé, unveiled at Geneva in 1966. This quickly made way for the Sonett V4 and then, in 1970, the restyled Sonett III. The 95 and 96 enjoyed exceptionally long careers, with

Saab's first estate car, the 95, was introduced in 1959.

Below: Erik Carlsson on his way to victory on the 1963 Monte-Carlo Rally with his two-stroke 96.

The final version of Saab's Sonett coupé, this Sonett III dates from 1972.

production of the 96 only coming to an end in 1980.

In the meantime, however, Saab had set its sights higher, and its next new model was the 99. Launched in 1968 as a medium-sized two-door saloon, it was initially powered by a 1.7-litre four-cylinder engine, developed jointly with Ricardo and Triumph in the UK. The range soon expanded to include a four-door saloon and then, in 1973, the iconic Combi Coupé, whose distinctive three-door design would continue with the 900 NG and first-generation 9-3 models until 2002. From 1977, the 99 was also the first Saab to be fitted with a turbocharged engine, which transformed the company's image.

In 1978, the 900 made its debut: it was similar in overall design to the 99, but extensively updated. Produced until 1994, the range included two- and four-door saloons, as well as three- and five-door coupés, with naturally aspirated or turbocharged petrol engines. For the first time, there was a convertible too. For many enthusiasts, the 900 'Classic' was Saab at its very best.

The three-door 99 Turbo, seen here in Pearlescent White.

A 900 GLE five-door from 1979.

A 9000 Turbo 16 from 1985.

Alongside the 900, in 1984 Saab moved further upmarket, when it introduced the 9000, developed as part of a platform-sharing agreement with Alfa Romeo, Fiat and Lancia.

The new-generation 900 NG was the first Saab released after GM stepped in.

Offered at first as a five-door hatchback, a four-door saloon was added later; engines included ever more powerful 2.0- and 2.3-litre turbocharged 'fours', as well as a short-lived V6.

Behind the scenes, however, all was not well, and in 1989, Saab lost over £200 million. The company was building too few cars, at too high a cost. Its product range was too limited, and the only successor to the 96 had been the ill-fated Saab-Lancia 600, a rebadged Lancia Delta. At the end of 1989, the ailing car division of the Saab-Scania group, which had merged in 1969, was spun off and GM acquired a 50 per cent stake in it.

A UK-registered Saab 9-5 2.2 TiD estate from 2002.

For many Saab fans, it was a dark day. The models that followed – the 900 NG (for new generation) in 1993 and the bigger 9-5 in 1997 – were based on GM's Opel Vectra platform. They nonetheless kept the Swedish firm's celebrated turbocharged engines and could still be recognised as Saabs. The 900 NG was probably released to market too soon and was replaced in 1998 by the first-generation 9-3: outwardly similar to the 900, the biggest changes were to the chassis, powertrain and body structure. Like its predecessor, it was sold as a five-door hatchback, three-door coupé and convertible.

With the 9-5, which replaced the 9000, Saab reintroduced an estate model to its range. Both the 9-3 and 9-5 were available with diesel engines, anathema to Saab purists, but essential for the company to be successful in Europe.

In January 2000, GM took full control of Saab, vowing to compete with the premium German brands and to save production and development costs. The next model to be launched, in 2002, was the second-generation 9-3, known as the Sport Saloon (or Sport Sedan in the US). It was a conventional four-door saloon, although a convertible was added to the range in 2003, followed by an estate in 2005. A 2.8-litre V6 turbo was available, as was four-wheel drive on some models. The 9-3 would remain in production until Saab went out of business.

The new 9-3 was well received by the press, but the same could not be said for GM's other attempts at extending the Saab brand during the 2000s. The Saab 9-2X was a rebadged Subaru Impreza, and the 9-7X a makeover of Chevrolet's TrailBlazer SUV. The 9-4X, a crossover based on the second-generation Cadillac SRX, would be the final offspring of this by-now unhappy union.

By 2009, not only was Saab doing badly, but so too was its GM parent. The Swedish company came within a hair's breadth of being closed down at the end of 2009 but enjoyed a brief stay of execution under the ownership of the Dutch firm Spyker Cars, before finally going into liquidation at the end of 2011.

Launched in 2009, the 9-3X was based on the 9-3 SportWagon and is shown here in 2.0T BioPower spec with four-wheel drive (XWD).

Saab went out in style, however, with the 9-5 NG, a superbly designed large saloon that went on sale in June 2010. Sadly, the magnificent estate version never made it into full-scale production. A handful of 9-3 models were later assembled by NEVS, which had acquired Saab's assets in 2012, but to all practical intents and purposes, 2011 marked the end of the line, after nearly 4.5 million Saabs had been built.

The 9-4X crossover.

Above: Spyker's exclusive sports cars, like this C8 Aileron Spyder, made unlikely bedfellows for Saab.

Left: The 9-5 NG would be Saab's swansong.

Acknowledgements

The majority of the photographs and other illustrations in this book were generously supplied by the Saab Car Museum or made available by Saab Automobile AB and Saab GB when the company was in business. Several other companies and individuals also kindly provided photographs for use here, and it is my pleasure to thank: Abbott Racing: page 103; Andrew Bannister (Car Brochure Addict): pages 60 (both), 61, 62 (both) and 63 (both); Bonhams|Cars: pages 7 (top), 12 (bottom), 15 (bottom), 16 (top), 18 (all), 21 (top), 25 (bottom), 27 (top), 30 (bottom), 32 (top), 34 (centre), 36 (bottom), 64 (top), 68 (bottom), 69 (bottom), 71 (bottom), 73 (top) and 74 (centre left & right, bottom); Jelger Groeneveld: page 36 (centre); Copyright Archives Maurice Louche: page 42 (bottom); Newspress UK: pages 10 (top), 11 (top), 79 (top), 104, 105 (both), 107 (top left, centre left & right), 133 (top) and 137 (top); Kevin Quinn: page 33 (bottom right); John Simister: page 25 (top), and Valmet Automotive: pages 34 (top) and 54 (bottom).

In writing this book, I have been able to draw on the road test archives of *Autocar*, *Le Moniteur Automobile*, *Car and Driver* and *Motor Sport* magazines, as well as Saab's original press releases. But nothing can replace the personal help of Saab's many fans, above all that of Peter Backström, the curator of the Saab Car Museum in Trollhättan.

Finally, my thanks are due once again to the team at Veloce Publishing, in particular Rod Grainger, who commissioned this title, Kevin Quinn – himself an enthusiastic Saab owner – and my editor, Becky Martin.

URSAAB, SAAB 92 AND 93

Saab established its reputation with a series of small, two-door saloons, beginning with the 92 in 1949. This evolved into the 93 and then the 96, but the overall styling and mechanical configuration remained the same. The saloons also spawned Saab's first estate car, the 95, a series of sports cars under the Sonett name and even a single-seat racing car and a caravan! All these models are described in this and the next two chapters.

DKW built more than 200,000 front-engined F-series cars at Zwickau from 1931–1942.

From Ursaab to production

During the 1930s, some of the most successful cars in Sweden had been those built by the German manufacturer DKW. They were well suited to the harsh conditions of Scandinavian winters, with their rugged construction and front-wheel drive, which was still rare at the time. They were smaller and cheaper than the cars produced by Volvo, which had been founded in 1927. Unsurprisingly therefore, Saab adopted many of the same design principles as DKW, and the first prototypes for the 92 were actually powered by DKW engines until Saab's own engines were ready.

Work began on Saab's planned new car during 1945 and a wooden model was ready in April 1946. Two months later, the first running prototype, 92.001, was shown to Saab's management and registered for the road soon afterwards. It became known in Swedish as the 'Ursaab' (or 'original Saab'). It was positioned below Volvo's larger models as a small car that would be light and easy to build and maintain, but faster and more economical than the prewar DKWs.

The Ursaab's radical aerodynamic design was the work of Sixten Sason. He had studied sculpture in Paris but was also a pilot and aircraft designer and even turned his hand to the design of Hasselblad cameras, Electrolux vacuum cleaners and Husqvarna motorbikes. Saab was unusual among car manufacturers at the time in having access to a wind tunnel, and the Ursaab had a remarkable drag coefficient of just 0.32, which rose only slightly, to 0.35, for the production 92. Its unique teardrop shape, known as 'Vingprofil' in Swedish, contributed to the car's stability in crosswinds, while its flat undertray further improved its aerodynamic efficiency.

With its all-steel monocoque construction, the new car was also

92.001, the very first prototype. Note the close-set headlamps under perspex fairings.

A model of the Ursaab undergoing testing in the wind tunnel at the Royal Institute of Technology in Stockholm in 1946.

This drawing of the Ursaab by Rony Lutz dates from 1947.

exceptionally strong. Its 15in wheels offered good ground clearance on rough roads, while the choice of front-wheel drive ensured good handling, especially in winter conditions. The absence of a central transmission tunnel also freed up more space inside the car.

For its ground-breaking car, Saab developed a new 764cc two-cylinder engine. A two-stroke unit, like those fitted to the DKWs, it had no inlet or exhaust valves and fewer moving parts. It was simple and cheap to build and easy to service, but needed to be revved to get decent performance and produced a good deal of blue smoke. The transversely mounted engine was mated to a three-speed transmission with a flywheel, which let the driver disengage the gears and coast to save fuel. The downside was the resultant lack of engine braking. Saab's first prototype engines were tested in pre-war DKWs and even entered in various competitive events, including the Skarpnäck Race in Stockholm in May 1948. This was won by Rolf Mellde, whom Saab had recruited to develop its new engine in September 1946.

Saab's two-cylinder engine, here fitted to a 1953 92B.

The second prototype, 92.002, with the revised frontal treatment and single-piece rear screen.

DKW's historic distributor in Sweden, Gunnar Philipson, was sufficiently convinced of the potential of the new model to commit to sell 8000 cars, the equivalent of three years' production. As the model numbers up to 91 were reserved for use on Saab's aircraft, the first available number was 92, a series that would continue through to the 99.

Following this promising start, work quickly ramped up on the new car. The second prototype, 92.002, which was unveiled to the world's press on 10 June 1947, had a more conventional nose with a less bulbous appearance, and the headlamps were farther apart. The rear screen was now a single-piece item rather than split. The original fully shrouded wheels also had to be modified for

In 1997, the Ursaab took to the road again, to celebrate its 50th birthday.

This drawing shows the original production 92, with access to luggage from inside the car and the fuel filler mounted in the tail panel.

production cars to prevent the build-up of mud and snow.

During the spring and summer of 1949, 20 pilot cars were built. Of these, two were Standard models (finished in dark blue) and 18 were Deluxe models (painted green). The Deluxe versions had bumpers, chrome rather than painted hub caps, a chrome-plated radiator grille and twin windscreen wipers, as well as much improved interior equipment including rear-seat armrests, an ashtray, heater, light-coloured steering wheel, clock and water temperature gauge. It was proposed that the two versions would be sold at 6180SEK and 6750SEK respectively. Philipson was opposed to the lower-spec Standard model, however, and it appears that all the Saab 92s actually built were Deluxe models. At first, all the cars were finished in bottle-green, quickly earning them the nicknames 'Jungle Drum' and 'Green Droplet'.

Saab 92 and 92B

Series production of the 92 began on 12 December 1949, and the first cars were delivered to customers in January 1950. Its weight of 765kg (1687lb) kept it in a lower tax band in Sweden, where it was priced below the Volvo PV444 and competed with cars like the Volkswagen Beetle and Renault 4CV. The motoring press congratulated Saab on the design of its new model.

Within weeks of its launch, the new Saab notched up its first win in competition, at a regional event in Östergötland. International successes soon followed, with Greta Molander taking second place in the Coupe des Dames on the 1950 Monte-Carlo Rally with chassis number 7. In 1953, Saab's own Rolf Mellde won the Swedish Rally Championship, and two years later a young Erik Carlsson scored his first major victory, on the tough Rikspokalen rally in Sweden.

Erik Carlsson and Sten Holm pressing on to victory on the 1955 Rikspokalen rally.

Installing the drivetrain in a 92 in Saab's factory in 1950.

Production of the 92 was held up in 1950 due to a shortage of steel and the need to modify the factory to install the new American presses Saab had bought. Throughout the 92's career, the company's focus was as much on building its production capacity as on steadily improving the cars.

Changes for 1952 were minor, with German VDO instruments replacing those supplied by the American firm Stewart-Warner. There was also now a chrome-plated Saab emblem on the dashboard.

December 1952 saw the biggest changes to the 92, when the 92B was launched. This had a 53 per cent larger rear screen and an opening boot lid: access to the luggage compartment had previously been by folding down the rear seat from inside the car, as on other saloon cars of the 1950s such as the Standard Eight. The rear seat itself could be removed and replaced by a large storage box or adapted for use as a makeshift bed. The fuel tank was also relocated, with the filler now on the left-hand rear wing.

The painted metal dashboard and light-coloured steering wheel of the 92.

The opening boot lid and larger rear screen can be clearly seen on this 1953 92B.

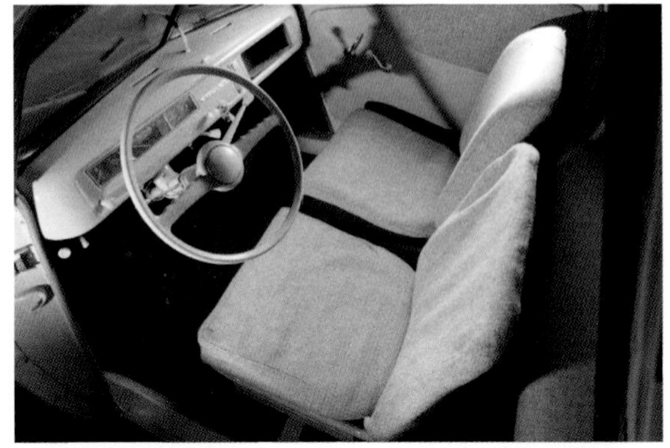

The interior of a 92B from 1953.

This 1954 92B sports the rare optional sunroof.

In 1954, power increased from 24 to 28bhp (net), thanks to the fitment of a Solex 32 BI carburettor and a new ignition coil. An electric fuel pump was added during the course of the year. Outside, the latest cars could be recognised by the chrome mouldings on both front and rear wings and the Plexiglas draught deflectors fitted to the doors. The range of colours was extended while, inside the car, the instrument panel was now illuminated and a fresh-air heating system fitted.

For 1955, as the 92 prepared to take its bow, the only change Saab made was to fit square rear lamps. Production of the 92 continued alongside the new 93 until the end of 1956, using the same one-piece bumpers fitted to the new model. Its influence would live on for many more years, however, with its basic shape still visible in the 96, which continued in production until 1980.

NUMBER PRODUCED: 20,152.
PRICE AT LAUNCH (SWEDEN): 6550SEK.
ENGINE: Transversely mounted two-cylinder, two-stroke petrol (with 4% oil mixture), valveless design with light-alloy cylinder head, water-cooled with thermosiphonic circulation system and no water pump. Single Solex 32 AIC carburettor (32 BI from 1954). **Bore:** 80mm; **stroke:** 76mm; **capacity:** 764cc. **Compression ratio:** 6.6:1; **maximum power:** 24bhp (net) at 3800rpm (28bhp at 4000rpm from 1954); **maximum torque:** 55Nm (41lb·ft).

By the time of this 1955 92B, maroon was one of the colours available. Note the chrome trim on the wings, added in 1954.

TRANSMISSION: Front-wheel drive, three-speed manual gearbox with column change and synchromesh on second and top, freewheel.
BRAKES: Lockheed hydraulic, drums at front and rear.
WHEELS & TYRES: 5.00 x 15in.
SUSPENSION: Independent, with transverse torsion bars and hydraulic shock absorbers at front and rear.
STEERING: Rack and pinion; **turning circle:** 11.0m (36ft).
ELECTRICAL SYSTEM: 6-volt Bosch.
DIMENSIONS: Length: 3.92m (154in); **width:** 1.62m (64in); **height:** 1.42m (56in); **wheelbase:** 2.47m (97in); **track (front & rear):** 1.17m (46in); **fuel tank:** 35 litres (7.75gal).
KERB WEIGHT: 765kg (1687lb).
PERFORMANCE FIGURES: Top speed: 68mph (110km/h); **0-50mph (80km/h):** 22sec; **overall fuel consumption:** 40mpg (7 litres/100km).
COLOURS: 1950–1952: green only.
1953: grey, blue-grey and black added.
1954: maroon added.
1955: grey, maroon, green.

Saab 93 and 93B

In just six years, the 92 established Saab's reputation as a car maker, and in December 1955 it presented its second model, logically named the 93. Its styling was an evolution of the 92, with more flowing lines (which still achieved a Cd figure of 0.35) and a completely new frontal appearance. With echoes of the Italian manufacturers Lancia and Alfa Romeo, it had a vertical radiator grille with smaller air intakes on either side. The single-piece chrome bumpers were new and there was a larger cut-out for the front wheels.

Inside, the 93 boasted improved upholstery and more comfortable seats, as well as a new steering wheel, gearlever and column-mounted indicator control. The instruments now included fuel and water temperature gauges, an ammeter and clock, together with a low fuel warning light. A manually operated blind behind the grille, for use in winter, was part of an improved 'Klimator' heating system. As on the 92, the seats could be folded down to make a bed or a storage box installed in place of the rear bench.

The biggest changes for the 93, however, were mechanical. A completely new three-cylinder engine with an alloy head, developed in collaboration with the German engineer Hans Müller, replaced the original twin. Now mounted longitudinally rather than transversely, it had a new cooling system, with a more conventional fan, thermostat and water pump, taking the place of the thermosiphonic system fitted to the 92. Slightly smaller in capacity than the engine in the 92, it developed 38bhp (net), a useful increase. The first 3000 engines were built by Heinkel in Germany, before Saab's new engine and gearbox factory in Gothenburg came online.

The gearbox, supplied by ZF, was also new, and the freewheel device could now be controlled by means of a knob under the dashboard rather than from under the bonnet. The torsion-bar suspension was replaced by coil springs, while the electrical system was upgraded from 6 to 12 volts. With safety already a key consideration for Saab, tubeless tyres reduced the risk of blowouts and the fuel tank was relocated between the rear wheels.

Two views of a 1957 Saab 93. The upright front and split windscreen can be clearly seen.

The three-cylinder engine fitted to the 93 was entirely new.

Saab's first model to be sold in the United States, the 93 was presented at the New York International Auto Show in the spring of 1956. In November that year, Saab claimed its first victory in competition in North America, when Bob Wehman and Louis Braun won the Great American Mountain Rally in New England. By the time the 93 went out of production in 1960, export sales accounted for 40 per cent of Saab's total output.

Back in Europe, Erik Carlsson soon adopted the new model, with a succession of

Rolf Mellde and Sverker Benson brought their 93 home in second place on the ADAC Tour d'Europe in 1956.

notable wins, including the Thousand Lakes Rally in Finland in 1957 and the Swedish Rally to the Midnight Sun in 1959. Driven by Charlie Lohmander and Harald Kronegård, the Saab 93 also won its class in the last ever edition of the great Mille Miglia race in 1957.

In April 1957, Saab introduced the Saxomat automatic clutch as an option on the 93. Produced by Fichtel & Sachs, it was offered on several other cars at the time, particularly from German manufacturers. It used a combination of centrifugal force, vacuum-servo and electromagnetic action to provide two-pedal driving. Two-point diagonal seatbelts also became available towards the end of 1957.

The 1958 model year saw the biggest changes to the 93, with the introduction of the 93B, first presented on 3 September 1957. Saab claimed "eleven important innovations" for the new model, the most noticeable of which was a single-piece windscreen, replacing the original split screen. Improved windscreen wipers with a parallel action ensured a 43 per cent increase in the swept area. There were improved door locks and additional chrome trim, while new indicators took the place of the antiquated semaphore indicators mounted on the door pillars. Under the bonnet, the most important change was the adoption of automatic mixing and the reduction of the oil mixture to three per cent. Improved brakes were also fitted.

This rather forced publicity shot of the 93B shows off the new single-piece windscreen.

Saab continued to promote its background in aviation, as in this photograph of a 93B next to a Saab J35 Draken fighter.

For 1959, Saab continued its policy of continuous improvement. The backrests of the new front seats could be adjusted to seven positions and there were more powerful brakes and asymmetrical headlamps. A windscreen washer was now standard, as was a driver's door mirror. The sun visors were padded for extra safety and the glove compartment was lockable. A feature we now take for granted, the interior lighting could be activated by opening the door.

1960 would be the 93's final model year, and in September 1959 Saab introduced the 93F, the letter 'F' denoting the new front-hinged doors, which would soon be found on the 95 and 96. The interior was a more comfortable place to spend time in, with new upholstery and door armrests. The capacity of the cooling system was also increased.

NUMBER PRODUCED: 52,731 (all models).
PRICE AT LAUNCH (SWEDEN): 7500SEK (including heater/demister).
ENGINE: Longitudinally mounted three-cylinder, two-stroke petrol (with 4% oil mixture, 3% with automatic mixing on 93B), valveless design with light-alloy cylinder head and four main bearings, water-cooled (with pump). Single Solex 40 AI carburettor and electric fuel pump. **Bore:** 66mm; **stroke:** 72.9mm; **capacity:** 748cc. **Compression ratio:** 7.3:1; **maximum power:** 38bhp (net) at 4200rpm; **maximum torque:** 68Nm (50lb·ft) at 3000rpm.
TRANSMISSION: Front-wheel drive, three-speed manual gearbox with column change

One last time: the model in this marketing shot is about to open the rear-hinged door of this 1959 93B.

The dashboard of a 1959 93B, with its new, lockable glove compartment. The non-standard steering wheel is similar to that on the Granturismo 750.

A 93F from 1960, Saab's first saloon to have front-hinged doors.

and synchromesh on second and top, freewheel. **Final drive ratio:** 5.73:1.
BRAKES: Lockheed hydraulic, drums at front and rear.
WHEELS & TYRES: 5.00 x 15in, tubeless tyres.
SUSPENSION: Front: independent, with double wishbones; **rear:** rigid U-shaped axle. Coil springs and telescopic shock absorbers at front and rear.
STEERING: Rack and pinion; **turning circle:** 11.0m (36ft).
ELECTRICAL SYSTEM: 12-volt; **battery capacity:** 33Ah.
DIMENSIONS: Length: 4.01m (158in); **width:** 1.57m (62in); **height:** 1.47m (58in); **wheelbase:** 2.49m (98in); **track (front & rear):** 1.22m (48in); **fuel tank:** 36 litres (8gal).
KERB WEIGHT: 810kg (1786lb).
PERFORMANCE FIGURES: Top speed: 75mph (120km/h); **0-50mph (80km/h):** 18sec; **overall fuel consumption:** 35mpg (8 litres/100km).

The red paint sets off the extra chrome trim and additional driving lights of this Granturismo 750 from 1959.

Granturismo 750

Keen to capitalise on its successes in rallying, for the first time Saab offered a sportier, high-performance model alongside the regular 93. Making its debut at the New York International Auto Show in April 1958, the Granturismo 750 was powered by a 50bhp (net) version of the 93's three-cylinder engine. For the GT 750 Super Sport variant, a tuning kit with twin Solex 44 carburettors further increased its power to 57.5bhp. To match the increased performance, bigger brakes, Pirelli Cinturato radial tyres, and a screen washer were fitted to all Granturismos.

Externally, the Granturismo 750 could be recognised by the dual bright trim strips on the lower part of the body, as well as larger chrome hub caps, dual door mirrors and additional driving lights. Inside, it was fully equipped, with a wood-rimmed steering wheel and rev counter for the driver, and a fully reclining seat with a headrest for the co-driver, who also had a grab handle to hang on to and a (Swedish-made) Halda Speed Pilot to operate. Front seatbelts were standard, a first on a production car.

Initially fitted with a three-speed manual gearbox, like the standard 93, the Granturismo 750 had a four-speed transmission from 1959, pre-empting the change that would later come to the 95 and 96. Some of the final cars also had the 93F body, with front-hinged doors. Altogether, only 605 Granturismo 750s were built from 1958-1960, the vast majority of which (an estimated 546) were exported to the US.

KEY DIFFERENCES

ENGINE: Single Solex 40 or, optionally, twin Solex 44 carburettors. **Maximum power:** 50bhp (net) at 5000rpm with single carburettor, or 57.5bhp (net) at 5500rpm with twin carburettors.

KERB WEIGHT: 865kg (1907lb).

PERFORMANCE FIGURES: Top speed: 84mph (135km/h) with single carburettor, or 93mph (150km/h) with twin carburettors.

SAAB 95 AND 96

The 94 model number had already been assigned to the Sonett roadster (see pages 39-41), so the first available numbers for Saab's next models were 95 and 96. When the 95 estate was presented at Linköping in May 1959, the 93 was still in production, but for most of its long career, the 95 was closely aligned with the 96 saloon. The very first 95s built in 1959 (fewer than 100) had rear-hinged side doors, but these were quickly changed to front-hinged doors, as fitted to the final 93F saloons and all 96s.

The 95 shared its 'bull nose' front with the 96.

The 95 was Saab's first estate model, with a three-door body style that had echoes of the Chevrolet Nomad. The 95 had a longer wheelbase than the 93, and offered much more space for luggage than the saloon, a particularly important consideration for Saab's customers in rural areas. Its modular seating layout enabled it to be configured as a two-seat van or as a five- or seven-seat family estate. The last row of seats faced rearwards and could be folded flat into the load floor. With both the middle and rearmost seats folded away, the 95 offered an uninterrupted load length of over 2m (79in). A panel van version was also sold in small numbers in some markets, including Denmark and Norway.

Introduced in February 1960, the 96 was a natural evolution of the 93. At launch, the doors were front-hinged, as on the final 93F models, and the frontal styling of the new car was very similar to the 93. These are often referred to as the 'bullnose' models, in contrast to the later 'long nose' versions. The rear of the 96, however, was completely new, with a rear screen that was more than

One of the very first 95s built in 1959, with rear-hinged side doors.

The foldaway rearward-facing seat in the luggage compartment of the 95 was best suited for use by children.

One of the rare panel van versions of the 95.

twice the size of that fitted to the 93. Air was extracted from the cabin through new vents behind decorative shields on the C pillars.

Inside, the 95 initially kept the dashboard from the 93, but the design for the 96 was entirely new, with four round dials (fuel and water temperature gauges, an ammeter and an eight-day clock) beneath a VDO strip speedometer, which read up to 90mph or 140km/h. On the 96, an accessory bed kit was still available as an option, as was a folding sunroof.

The engine powering the 95 and 96 was a new 841cc unit developing 42bhp (SAE), which retained the three-cylinder two-stroke design of the engine fitted to the 93. The 96 launched with the company's familiar three-speed gearbox, but for the first time, the 95 had a four-speed all-synchromesh gearbox, an improvement long requested by Saab owners. The 95 was understandably heavier than the 93, but the additional gear ratio helped make the most of the available performance, especially when allied to the cars' agile handling. Both transmissions had Saab's traditional freewheel and a column gear change.

The 95 and 96 models were the first Saabs to be officially imported and sold in the UK, and the cars premièred at the London Motor Show in autumn 1960. Saab GB was set up by Squadron Leader Robert Moore, who had been a test pilot for Saab (flying the Saab 29 Tunnan fighter) after the war. Priced at

The side air vents and larger rear screen of the 96 can be seen in this marketing shot.

The new dashboard fitted to the 96 at launch.

£885, including purchase tax, at launch in the UK, the 96 was expensive and competed with cars from the class above it, but the quality of its design and engineering and its excellent build quality were recognised by the press.

It should be no surprise that the 96 should continue Saab's winning streak in rallying. Erik Carlsson was at his peak, claiming victory in the RAC Rally in 1960, 1961 and 1962 and the Monte-Carlo in 1962 and 1963. With other great drivers including Pat Moss (Carlsson's wife), Per Eklund, Carl-Magnus Skogh, Simo Lampinen and Stig Blomqvist, the 96 also chalked up wins in its class and overall in countless other events, including the Acropolis Rally in Greece, the Thousand Lakes Rally in Finland and the Swedish Rally to the Midnight Sun. Even the 95 saw some action

The 841cc two-stroke engine installed in a 95 from 1961.

Erik Carlsson and Pat Moss hoping for another victory on the Monte Carlo Rally in 1964.

in competition, and Erik Carlsson finished the 1961 Monte-Carlo Rally fourth with a 95.

For 1961, the starter was now operated by the ignition key on both the 95 and 96, and in March that year the 95 gained one of its most distinctive features: the wind deflector mounted at the top of the rear screen to keep it clear. The 95 also received the new dashboard design that had been introduced when the 96 launched, and production was transferred to Trollhättan.

From August 1961 the wheels of the 96 were painted silver with all body colours. The following year, a four-speed gearbox became available in some markets, before being progressively standardised over the next couple of years.

At the end of 1961, diagonal front seatbelts were fitted to all 95s and 96s in Sweden (the exact date of introduction in export markets varied by country).

In February 1962, Saab responded to the continuing success of the 96 in competition by introducing the higher-performance model known as the Granturismo 850 in the US and as the Saab Sport in the UK. This is described more fully in the next section.

For the 1963 models, the Saab badge on both the 95 and 96 moved from the top of the bonnet to the radiator grille. The other improvements were chiefly inside the car: the seats were now higher, the heating and ventilation system was improved and there was a new horn ring and a larger rear-view mirror.

For 1964, diagonal dual-circuit brakes were fitted to both the saloon and estate, marking another major contribution to safety by Saab, and the ignition lock now also locked

The rear screen deflector was first fitted to the 95 in 1961, the year of this model.

the gearlever in reverse, a feature historically associated with the marque. Inside both the 95 and 96, there was a new dashboard with three round dials, but an ammeter was no longer included.

The first major facelift for the 95 and 96 came in 1965, when the so-called 'long nose' design with a wider front grille was introduced. The cooling system was updated and the radiator was now positioned in front of the engine. Power increased to 44bhp (SAE) and there were numerous other mechanical improvements, with a new fuel pump, exhaust system and hydraulically-operated clutch. The lubrication intervals were extended to 6250mi (10,000km) to reduce the cost of ownership.

1966 saw some of the final changes to the two-stroke engine: a new carburettor and induction system added 2bhp and the oil mixture was reduced to 1.5 per cent. The three-speed manual gearbox had completely disappeared in manual form, although the Saxomat automatic clutch remained available in combination with the three-speed transmission in the 96. The pedals were now of the conventional top-hung type.

NUMBER PRODUCED: 95 (all models): 110,527; 96 (all models) 547,221.
PRICE AT LAUNCH (UK – 96): £885, including purchase tax.
ENGINE: Longitudinally-mounted three-cylinder, two-stroke petrol (with 3% oil mixture, 1.5% from 1966), valveless design, water-cooled. Single Solex 40 BI carburettor. **Bore:** 70mm, **stroke:** 72.9mm, **capacity:** 841cc.

The original position of the Saab badge on the 95 and 96 was above the radiator grille.

From 1963, the badge moved down to the grille itself and incorporated aircraft propellors in its design.

One of the first 'long nose' 96 models, introduced in 1965.

Compression ratio: 7.3:1; **maximum power:** 42bhp (SAE) at 4250rpm (increased to 44bhp (SAE) from 1965); **maximum torque:** 80Nm (59lb·ft) at 3000rpm.
TRANSMISSION: Front-wheel drive, four-speed all-synchromesh manual gearbox (three-speed gearbox on 96 until 1962/64 depending on market) with column change and freewheel. Saxomat automatic clutch optional with three-speed transmission on 96 only. **Final drive ratio:** 5.43:1.
BRAKES: Lockheed hydraulic, drums at front and rear. Diagonal split circuit from 1964.
WHEELS & TYRES: 5.20 x 15in.
SUSPENSION: Front: independent, with double wishbones, coil springs and telescopic shock absorbers; **rear:** rigid U-shaped axle, coil springs and telescopic shock absorbers (96)/lever-arm shock absorbers (95).
STEERING: Rack and pinion; **turning circle:** 11.2m (37ft).
ELECTRICAL SYSTEM: 12-volt; **battery capacity:** 33Ah.
DIMENSIONS: Length: 96 'bull nose': 4.05m (159in), 96 'long nose': 4.20m (165in), 95 'bull nose': 4.11m (162in), 95 'long nose': 4.30m (169in); **width:** 1.58m (62in); **height:** 1.45m (57in); **wheelbase:** 2.49m (98in); **track (front & rear):** 1.22m (48in); **fuel tank:** 40 litres (8.8gal).
KERB WEIGHT: 96: 816kg (1799lb; 95: 905kg (1995lb).
LOAD CAPACITY (95): 1200 litres (42.4ft3) with all seats folded; **payload:** 500kg (1102lb).
PERFORMANCE FIGURES (96): Top speed: 76mph (122km/h); **0-60mph (96km/h):** 24.1sec; **overall fuel consumption:** 26-28mpg (10.8-12.8 litres/100km).
COLOURS:
1960-1964: Toreador Red, Polar White, Midnight Blue, Savannah Brown, Glacier Blue.

Granturismo 850/Saab Sport

Saab's first high-performance version of the 96 was in fact a temporary continuation of the GT 750, which was fitted with the 96 body from autumn 1960, but kept the 748cc engine from the 93.

It was at the Stockholm Motor Show in February 1962 that Saab introduced the true successor to the GT 750, known as the Granturismo 850 in the US and as the Saab Sport in the UK. The launch of the right-hand drive Saab Sport was delayed in the UK, however, and as an interim measure Saab GB produced its own limited series of 56 modified cars, dubbed the Saab 60, in 1962/63. The engine, mated to a four-speed gearbox, was uprated to 60bhp (SAE), so giving the model its name; a sports exhaust was also fitted, and the suspension lowered.

Like the GT 750, the Granturismo 850/ Saab Sport was better equipped, with additional driving lights, a wood-rimmed steering wheel, rev counter and passenger headrest. It proved very thirsty, however, and when it reached the UK, it was more expensive than Ford's Cortina GT, which easily outperformed it, both factors that cost it sales.

The Granturismo 850 had the same three-cylinder 841cc engine as the standard 96, but with three parallel-linked Solex carburettors, boosting power to 52bhp (DIN), and a three-litre oil tank with automatic petrol/ oil mixing. For the first time on the 96, it had a four-speed transmission, still with a column gear change, but with synchromesh on all

This 1963 model had a 'Saab Sport' badge on its front wing.

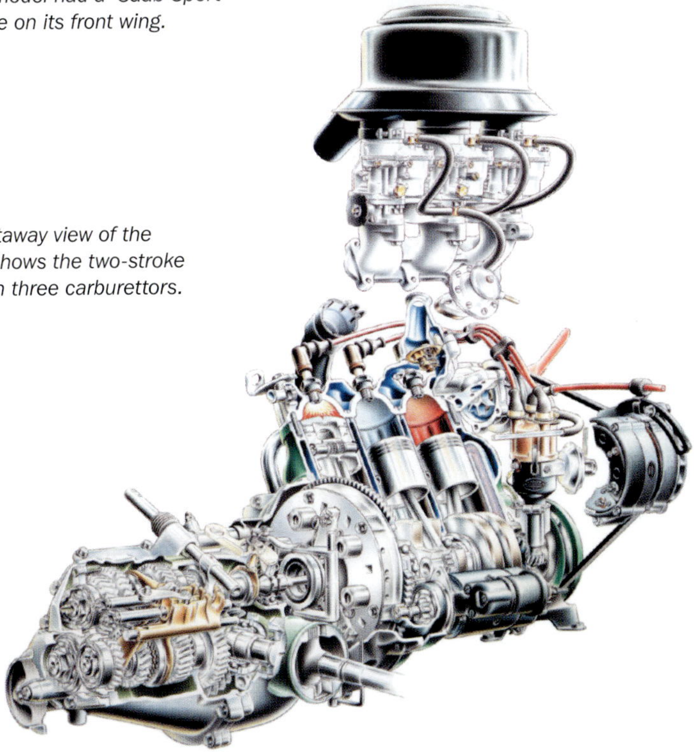

This cutaway view of the drivetrain shows the two-stroke engine with three carburettors.

four forward speeds. Front disc brakes and a diagonal split circuit ensured improved braking to match the higher performance.

For 1963, the Granturismo 850/Saab Sport was fitted with a new dashboard with a full complement of round instruments.

In 1965, power went up to 55bhp (DIN) and an alternator was fitted. The model was renamed the Monte Carlo in the US, as a tribute to Erik Carlsson's victories on the event. The Monte Carlo name was then extended to all markets from 1966.

With the arrival of the V4 engine, the three-cylinder engine was outclassed, and in January 1967 the V4 engine was standardised on the Monte Carlo, but it had the same power output as the regular model and only remained on sale for another year.

KEY DIFFERENCES

PRICE (UK – 1965): £1139, including purchase tax.
ENGINE: Three Solex 34 downdraught carburettors. **Compression ratio:** 9.0:1, **maximum power:** 55bhp (DIN) at 5000rpm, **maximum torque:** 91Nm (67lb·ft) at 3800rpm.
TRANSMISSION: Four-speed all-synchromesh manual gearbox with column change and freewheel. **Final drive ratio:** 5.14:1.
BRAKES: **Front:** discs; **rear:** drums. Diagonal split circuit.
WHEELS & TYRES: Pirelli Cinturato 155-section radial-ply tyres.
ELECTRICAL SYSTEM: 12-volt; **battery capacity:** 54Ah.
KERB WEIGHT: 880kg (1940lb).
PERFORMANCE FIGURES: **Top speed:** 88mph (142km/h); **0-60mph (96km/h):** 19.1sec; **overall fuel consumption:** 21mpg (13.4 litres/100km).

By 1966, the Monte Carlo model name was in use in all markets. Note the passenger headrest and extra driving lights.

A Monte Carlo prepared for rallying, with the bumpers removed and Minilite-type wheels fitted.

95 and 96 V4

Saab's senior management sometimes remained wedded to its traditional solutions for too long, and that was certainly the case for the original engines fitted to the 95 and 96. By the mid-1960s, there were few manufacturers left outside Eastern Europe who persisted with two-stroke engines.

Saab's engineers, however, were convinced that the company had to have a more modern, four-stroke, four-cylinder engine for the 95 and 96 to remain competitive. As Saab had too little money to develop a new engine itself, Rolf Mellde and his team looked at a range of four-cylinder units from Borgward, BMC, Lancia and Opel, among others. In the end, however, they settled on the 1.5-litre V4 developed by Ford of Germany for its Taunus 15m model. The engine was tested in great secrecy in a rented villa in Italy by a small team led by Mellde and Per Gillbrand. Although the results were conclusive, Mellde had to go over the head of his CEO and appeal directly to the Wallenberg family, Saab's main shareholders, for the project to be approved.

In any event, the arrival of the two V4 models in August 1966 was welcomed by the company's customers. The V4 was a slightly coarse but torquey engine, which offered far better performance and improved fuel consumption into the bargain.

The 96 V4 was initially advertised as an extra model, and in Europe it soon supplanted the two-stroke models. In the US, however, two versions remained on sale until 1968 with the two-stroke engine: the so-called 'Shrike' model, with petrol/oil mixing and a reduced capacity of 819cc (to circumvent US emissions regulations) and the Saab 'Auto-Lube Sedan' with a separate oil tank.

Production of the 96, in particular, increased substantially, from 29,766 in 1966 to 37,622 in 1967, the first full year in which the V4 was available. The final two-stroke engines were built in 1968.

The arrival of the V4 engine also gave the 96 a fresh impetus in competition, which continued until 1975, when it took the top three places in the Arctic Rally. The 1.7-litre version of the V4, fitted to US-market cars from 1971, could be enlarged further to 1740 or 1815cc, allowing it to be homologated in the two-litre class. It was typically fitted with twin Weber sidedraught carburettors, producing as much as 155-175bhp. Drawing on its success in rallying, Saab marketed a tuning kit for the V4 and a wide range of performance and competition parts for private customers.

In 1967, front disc brakes were fitted as standard to both the 95 and 96 V4, and the electrical system was substantially improved, with an alternator, larger-capacity battery and more powerful starter motor. Inside, three-point front seatbelts were fitted, together with new upholstery and detachable storage bins mounted on the front wheelarches.

The changes made to the 95 and 96 for the 1968 model year focused on the cars' appearance and improving their safety rather than their mechanical specification. The front screen was larger and the dashboard and controls were now finished in dark grey and black respectively to avoid reflections, while a safety pad was added to the (now larger) steering wheel. The rear window of the 96 was also enlarged and a Deluxe version of the saloon became available, with extra trim, stainless steel window surrounds, radial-ply

A V4 badge was fitted to the front wing of the 96 V4.

The V4 engine, seen here in a 96 from 1976.

tyres and reversing lights. This remained on sale until 1970.

For 1969, the frontal styling of the 95 and 96 changed again, with the adoption of rectangular headlamps (except in the US, where round, sealed-beam headlamps were mandatory) set into a new chrome grille. The front bumper was mounted higher and had additional rubber-faced overriders. For the first time, the brakes had power assistance, while there was a new Autolite carburettor and air filter. During 1969, a new assembly plant was opened by Valmet at Uusikaupunki in Finland.

For 1970, the dashboard design was changed once again, with a more modern all-black design housing two round dials. The following year, the 95 and 96 gained a rubber side moulding and the chrome trip strips over the wheelarches were dropped.

In order to meet increasingly stringent emission regulations, for 1971 the engine capacity on cars destined for the US market was increased to 1.7 litres, although the power output remained unchanged at 65bhp (DIN). In Europe, headlamp wipers and washers became available on both the 95/96 and 99,

This 96 V4 has been equipped for rallying, with headlamp guards, extra driving lights and sump protection.

A 96 V4 Deluxe outside the fashionable Meeths department store in Stockholm.

This grey dashboard with three round dials and a centre pad on the steering wheel was introduced for 1968 on both the 95 and 96 V4.

Rectangular headlamps were fitted to both the 95 and 96 (outside the US) from 1969.

another Saab innovation that was particularly appreciated in Swedish winter conditions.

The 95 and 96 still had several years to run, and there was a succession of changes to the cars' appearance and specification throughout the 1970s. In 1972, an electrically heated, thermostatically controlled driver's

Employees at Valmet's plant in Finland celebrate 50 years since the first 96 was produced there.

This design of dashboard with two round dials was fitted throughout the 1970s.

For 1971, Saab introduced headlamp wipers on the 95/96 and 99.

The final design of radiator grille, made from black plastic.

seat became available, followed a year later by standard-fit halogen headlamps in European markets. Cars built for the 1974 model year onwards could be identified by their new frontal design with a black plastic radiator grille; radial-ply tyres and inertia-reel front seatbelts were fitted as standard, with inertia-reel rear seatbelts an option in some markets from 1975. A strengthened gearbox was also fitted in 1975.

For 1975, to celebrate 25 years since the Saab 92 went on sale, a limited series of 300 Silver Jubilee models was introduced. All the cars were finished in Silver Crystal Metallic and had side stripes, black C-pillar vents and special orange and brown interior trim. A special SE-spec 1.7-litre V4 was also offered, with alloy wheels, a rev counter and a leather-trimmed steering wheel.

In line with the changes seen on many cars at this time, in 1976 the 95 and 96 were fitted with black impact-absorbent safety bumpers, which arguably did little to improve the cars' now increasingly dated looks. On the 95, the famous rear-facing third row of seats was discontinued as the fuel tank was relocated to give increased legroom in the middle row.

An electric heated rear window and head restraints became standard in several markets, and daylight running lights (DRLs) made their first appearance in the cars' home market. The two models were now known as 95L and 96L. The power output of the 1.5-litre V4 decreased from 65 to 62bhp (DIN).

By 1977, the end of the road for the 95 and 96 was approaching, and they were withdrawn from sale in some countries. New front seats with integrated head restraints, like those fitted to the 99, were now fitted to the 96 (with the 95 following suit a year later), there were new textile carpets, black-finished exterior mirrors and twin chrome strips on the rubber bumpers. During the course of the year, a different, two-stage Solex carburettor was fitted and power went back up to 68bhp (DIN), earning these cars a 'V4 Super' badge at the rear.

The 1978 model year cars – now known as the 95 and 96 GL, following the naming convention applied to the 99 – benefitted from larger front indicators and taillamps, along with a rubber boot lid handle-cum-tail spoiler on the saloon.

A late-model 95 with impact-absorbent safety bumpers and headlamp wipers.

Twin chrome trim strips were added to the rubber bumpers on this 1977 model 96L.

In 1973, Saab had successfully launched the 99 Combi Coupé and therefore looked at applying the same stylistic treatment to the 95 to extend its life. Björn Envall designed a three-door prototype, to be known as the 98, built on the floorpan of the 95; it was assembled by Sergio Coggiola, who had also worked on the Sonett III coupé. In the end, Saab decided not to put the car into production and a single example survives, at the Saab Car Museum in Trollhättan.

Production of the 95 came to an end in February 1978, leaving the 96 to continue for another two years. In the UK, the final 150 right-hand drive saloons were sold in 1978 as a limited series of 96L 'Souvenir' models, all finished in Cardinal Red metallic paint and with a numbered plate on the dashboard.

The sole remaining Saab 98 prototype, finished in Sienna Brown.

For 1979, the 96 models – all now built at Uusikaupunki in Finland – had numerous black trim details, including the window surrounds and panel between the taillamps.

One of the final UK-market 96L 'Souvenir' models.

The very last 96 went directly to Saab's museum in Trollhättan.

The wheels had simple black centre caps as standard (with no hubcaps), but Minilite and 99 EMS-style 'soccer ball' alloy wheels were available as extras.

The last 96 saloon left the production line in Finland in January 1980, 30 years after the original 92 had been introduced. The model bowed out with a special series of 300 Aquamarine Blue cars, all fitted with Minilite wheels and see-through head restraints.

PRICE AT LAUNCH (UK – 96 V4): £801, including purchase tax.
ENGINE: Longitudinally-mounted 60-degree V4, four-stroke petrol, OHV layout with three main bearings, water-cooled. Single Solex 32 or Autolite carburettor. **Bore:** 90mm; **stroke:** 58.9mm (1.7-litre version: 66.8mm); **capacity:** 1498cc (1698cc from 1971 in US). **Compression ratio:** 9.0:1; **maximum power:** 65bhp (DIN) at 4700rpm; **maximum torque:** 115Nm (85lb·ft) at 2500rpm.
TRANSMISSION: Front-wheel drive, four-speed all-synchromesh manual gearbox with column change and freewheel. **Final drive ratio:** 4.88:1.
BRAKES: Front: discs (from 1967); **rear:** drums. Diagonal split circuit.
WHEELS & TYRES: 5.20 x 15in at launch, 155 SR 15 radial-ply tyres standard from 1974.
SUSPENSION: Front: independent, with double wishbones, coil springs and telescopic shock absorbers; **rear:** rigid U-shaped axle, coil springs and telescopic shock absorbers (96)/lever-arm shock absorbers (95).
STEERING: Rack and pinion, **turning circle:** 10.6m (35ft).
ELECTRICAL SYSTEM: 12-volt; **battery capacity:** 44Ah.
DIMENSIONS: Length: 96 V4 with chrome bumpers: 4.20m (165in), 95 V4 with chrome bumpers: 4.30m (169in), add 11cm (4in) for rubber bumpers; **width:** 1.59m (62in); **height:** 96 V4: 1.47m (58in), 95 V4: 1.49m (59in); **wheelbase:** 2.49m (98in); **track (front & rear):** 1.22m (48in); **fuel tank:** 40 litres (8.8gal).
KERB WEIGHT: 96 V4: 890kg (1962lb), 95 V4: 955kg (2105lb).
LOAD CAPACITY (95 V4): 1200 litres (42.4ft^3) with all seats folded; **maximum payload:** 500kg (1102lb).
PERFORMANCE FIGURES (96 V4): Top speed: 92mph (148km/h); **0-60mph (96km/h):** 16.5sec; **overall fuel consumption:** 29mpg (9.7/100km).
COLOURS (1972): Verona Green, Polar White, Mellanblå (Blue), Burgundy Red, Ambra (Yellow), Tyrol Green, Toreador Red.

Saab Formula Junior racing car

Rolf Mellde at the wheel of the Saab Formula Junior. Only one of the two cars built had these reinforcing ribs.

One of the most surprising offshoots of the programme to develop the 95 and 96, the Saab Formula Junior was designed by Rolf Mellde as a testbed for the new engine. The single-seat racer had an advanced alloy-monocoque construction with glass-fibre front and rear body sections. The whole car weighed less than 400kg (880lb).

The Formula Junior remained true to Saab's preferred front-wheel drive layout, but the engine was laid on its side and positioned ahead of the front axle. This resulted in a 70:30 weight distribution, causing drastic understeer. The suspension was similar to that fitted to Saab's production cars, but used coil springs working under tension rather than compression.

The engine itself was derived from the 841cc three-cylinder two-stroke, but was bored out to 950cc. With a double Solex downdraught carburettor and twin electric fuel pumps, power was estimated at 95-100bhp at 7000rpm.

Two cars were built in 1960 and they competed at eight races in Scandinavia during the 1961 season, driven mainly by Saab's rallymen Carl-Magnus Skogh and Erik Carlsson. They achieved mixed results, but finished first and second in the final Swedish championship race.

SaabO caravan

Beginning with the 92, Saab offered an accessory bed kit, enabling its owners to sleep overnight in their cars. But with the SaabO, it went a step further by creating a small trailer caravan. A seemingly far-fetched addition to Saab's product range, it came about as an unofficial project devised by two of the company's engineers, who were looking for a product to make use of the spare capacity in its helicopter plant. After showing a 1/10 scale model to Saab's management, the project was approved and from 1964-1968 about 400 SaabO caravans were built at its plant in Ljunga.

Officially named the Typ 260-3, the SaabO was constructed from two half-shells of glass-reinforced plastic (GRP). It was designed for a family of four or five and had an unusual front window, positioned low down so that the driver could see through the caravan in the rear-view mirror when towing. Inside, it had two sofa-beds, a dining table and basic galley.

It was kept as light as possible, so that it could be towed easily by small cars. The first 50 units built had no brakes, as these were not yet mandatory in Sweden.

PRICE AT LAUNCH (SWEDEN): 4950SEK
DIMENSIONS: Length: 3.60m (142in) with hitch; **width:** 1.84m (72in); **exterior height:** 2.10m (83in); **interior headroom:** 1.80m (71in).
KERB WEIGHT: 230-290kg (507-639lb).

The low-set front window and two-part construction of the SaabO can be seen in this period photograph.

SAAB SONETT I, II, V4 AND III

Some of the most appealing – and unusual – cars to come out of Trollhättan in Saab's early years were the Sonett models. The name was first used on a prototype roadster in the mid-1950s, before returning for the production coupés built from 1966-1974.

Saab 94: Sonett I

The 92 and 93 saloons did well in rallying, but for circuit racing Saab needed a lighter car. It was a point not lost on Rolf Mellde, Saab's engineering lead and a keen amateur racer. Saab's management was initially sceptical and Mellde began work on the project in secret, in a barn away from the Trollhättan factory, while Sixten Sason contributed to the design of its body. The name 'Sonett' – reputedly derived from the Swedish phrase "Så nätt den är" (it's so neat) – had originally been proposed for the 92 back in 1947. It was also known as the Super Sonett and the Type 94, following on from the 92 and 93 saloons.

In the end, however, Saab's bosses liked the prototype – an open two-seater designed strictly for competition – and it was well received by the press at the Stockholm Motor Show in March 1956 and in New York the following month.

The body – which weighed only 71kg (157lb) – was constructed from glass-fibre laminate and built over a box-shaped aluminium frame. It had a distinctive appearance, with a low-set radiator and small tailfins to improve its aerodynamic efficiency.

The suspension was similar to that of the 93, but with shorter coil springs at the front. In other respects, the car was mechanically similar to the 93, but the compression ratio of the two-stroke engine was raised to 10.0:1 and power increased to 57.5bhp (net). Twin water pumps and dual thermostats were fitted to help with cooling.

The layout of the engine and transmission, however, was quite different to the 93, with the engine turned through 180 degrees and positioned behind the four-speed ZF gearbox (and so behind the front axle), in order to improve weight distribution. The first two prototypes had a three-speed transmission, but on the later cars, the gearbox was a four-speed ZF unit, with the gearlever mounted in an open gate on the doorsill. The overall weight of the car was estimated at only 500kg (1102lb).

In November 1956, ASJ in Linköping was contracted to build five more prototypes. Over the next 12 months, two sets of plans were drawn up to put the car into series production. The first proposal was for Jensen in the UK

Since Sweden drove on the left until September 1967, all the Sonett prototypes had right-hand drive.

The small tailfins are clearly visible in this view of the blue prototype.

The dashboard was unique to the Sonett, with round dials including a large speedometer and rev counter. Note too the sill-mounted gearlever.

(which was also responsible for the first Volvo P1800 coupés) to build the car, but the discussions did not work out. Saab then looked at producing the Sonett in-house at Trollhättan, with an aluminium body and a folding hood. In the end, however, it considered the car too expensive to produce, and decided to concentrate instead on the Granturismo 750.

The Sonett's career in motor racing was ultimately brief, as it competed for only a single season, in 1957. It nonetheless won its first race (at Karlskoga, driven by Erik Carlsson) and its last (with Erik Lundgren at the wheel).

NUMBER PRODUCED: 6.
ENGINE: Longitudinally-mounted three-cylinder, two-stroke petrol, valveless design with light-alloy cylinder head and four main bearings, water-cooled (with pump). Solex PII double carburettor and electric fuel pump. **Bore:** 66mm; **stroke:** 72.9mm; **capacity:**

The Sonett returned to the track in 1997, to celebrate its 40th anniversary.

748cc. **Compression ratio:** 10.0:1; **maximum power:** 57.5bhp (net) at 5000rpm; **maximum torque:** 88Nm (65lb·ft) at 3500rpm.
TRANSMISSION: Front-wheel drive, three-speed manual gearbox with synchromesh on second and top on first two cars; four-speed 'box on later cars, sill-mounted gear change, freewheel.
BRAKES: Hydraulic, drums at front and rear.
WHEELS: 15in.
SUSPENSION: Front: independent; **rear:** rigid straight axle. Coil springs and telescopic shock absorbers at front and rear.
STEERING: Rack and pinion; **turning circle:** 11.0m (36ft).
ELECTRICAL SYSTEM: 12-volt; **battery capacity:** 33Ah.
DIMENSIONS: Length: 3.49m (137in); **width:** 1.42m (56in); **height:** 0.83m (33in); **wheelbase:** 2.21m (87in); **track (front & rear):** 1.22m (48in); **fuel tank:** 36 litres (8gal).
KERB WEIGHT: 500kg (1102lb).
PERFORMANCE FIGURES: Top speed (open version): 99mph (160km/h); **claimed top speed for closed version:** 124mph (200km/h); **0-62mph (100km/h):** 12sec; **overall fuel consumption:** 28mpg (10 litres/100km).

Saab 97: Sonett II, V4 and III

During the years that followed the first Sonett prototype, the global sports car market evolved considerably. In the late 1950s and early 1960s, British manufacturers such as MG, Triumph and Jaguar sold all the sports cars they could build in North America. Meanwhile, the US became an increasingly important territory for Saab, buoyed by its impressive results in competition.

One American enthusiast, Walter Kern, went so far as to build a series of Saab-based sports and racing cars under the Quantum name. In 1962, his Quantum III roadster attracted the interest of Saab USA. Saab

Sixten Sason's 'Catherina' prototype from 1965.

The original Sonett II from 1966 was the purest looking: note the chrome bonnet locks, wooden dashboard, roll bar and rear boot opening.

turned down a proposal from Kern to take on the car, but a seed had been planted.

In the end, two completely different prototypes were created before Saab committed to producing the Sonett II. The first, known as the 'Catherina', was designed by Sixten Sason in his private studio, and had a Targa-type roof. Despite being well received when shown to the public in Linköping, it was considered too expensive to build; its weight and poor aerodynamics also counted against it.

The second prototype, codenamed the MFI 13, was the work of the designer Björn Karlström. Also based on Saab 96 mechanicals, it was built by Malmö Flygindustri, which had some experience in manufacturing plastic components. Karlström took his proposal to Saab, who approved the proposal in May 1965 and quickly adapted it for production, assigning it the model number 97. Known commercially as the Sonett II, it was formally launched at the Geneva Motor Show in March 1966.

Sonett II

A two-seat coupé, the Sonett II's fibreglass body was moulded in two sections, with a roll bar to increase its strength. It had a minimal rear overhang and a Kamm tail (with access to the boot by means of a vertical panel below the rear screen). Inside was an elegant wood-veneer dashboard, like those often found on British sports cars. All Sonett II, V4 and III cars built had left-hand drive.

The mechanical specification of the Sonett II was very similar to the 96 Monte Carlo, but with different Solex carburettors, lifting its power to 60bhp (DIN). In September 1966, two Sonett IIs competed in the Coupe des Alpes (Alpine Rally); entered in the prototype

Elisabeth Nyström (L) and Pat Moss (R) taking a break beside their Sonett II on the 1966 Coupe des Alpes.

Erik Carlsson at the wheel of a Sonett II with rubber bonnet latches and the later style of radiator grille and Saab badge.

class, their engines were bored out to 940cc and produced 92bhp.

For 1967, the Sonett II received a new radiator grille with horizontal bars, there was a Saab badge on the bonnet and the chrome bonnet locks (similar to those used by Triumph) were replaced by rubber latches mounted lower down.

NUMBER PRODUCED: 258.
ENGINE: Three-cylinder 841cc petrol, as fitted to 96 Monte Carlo (see data for Granturismo 850/Saab Sport on page 30), but with three Solex 40 DHW carburettors. **Compression ratio:** 10.0:1; **maximum power:** 60bhp (DIN) at 5200rpm; **maximum torque:** 93Nm (69lb·ft) at 4000rpm. **Californian-market cars:** 803cc 'Shrike' engine with direct oil injection.
TRANSMISSION: Front-wheel drive, four-speed all-synchromesh manual gearbox with column change and freewheel. **Final drive ratio:** 4.88:1.
BRAKES: Front: discs; **rear:** drums. Lockheed diagonal dual-circuit hydraulic system.
WHEELS & TYRES: 4J x 15in.
SUSPENSION: Front: independent, with double wishbones, coil springs and telescopic shock absorbers; **rear:** rigid U-shaped axle, coil springs and telescopic shock absorbers.
STEERING: Rack and pinion; **turning circle:** 9.6m (32ft).
ELECTRICAL SYSTEM: 12-volt; **battery capacity:** 33Ah.
DIMENSIONS: Length: 3.76m (148in); **width:** 1.50m (59in); **height:** 1.16m (46in); **wheelbase:** 2.15m (85in); **track (front & rear):** 1.22m (48in); **fuel tank:** 60 litres (13.2gal).
KERB WEIGHT: 780kg (1720lb).
PERFORMANCE FIGURES: Top speed: 93mph (150km/h); **0-62mph (100km/h):** 12.5sec.

Sonett V4

The Sonett II's career was short-lived, however, as in the summer of 1967, it was replaced by the Sonett V4, powered by the same 1.5-litre Ford V4 fitted to the 95 and 96 V4 models. This delivered similar performance to the two-stroke version, but was less temperamental and easier to drive.

The new model could easily be identified by its bonnet bulge (sporting a Sonett V4 badge) needed to provide extra space for the new engine, as well as air outlets behind the doors and overriders on the front bumpers. The dashboard now had a black crinkled finish.

In 1969, new seats with integrated head restraints and lumbar cushions were fitted, and there was a new leather-wrapped steering wheel and a lid for the glove box.

KEY DIFFERENCES

NUMBER PRODUCED: 1613.
PRICE (US – 1968): $3695.
ENGINE: 1498cc V4 petrol, as fitted to 95 and 96 V4 (see page 37).

The advent of the V4 engine forced Saab's designers to adopt this ungainly bonnet bulge.

Sonett III

The looks of the Sonett V4 attracted some criticism and Saab's management realised that the car needed a more thorough redesign to sustain its career. The company rejected a proposal by Björn Andreasson at Malmö Flygindustri (which was now owned by Saab) to transform the Sonett into a 2+2 coupé and the project was instead entrusted to the Italian stylist Sergio Coggiola. His original design was, however, too wide for the existing Sonett chassis without making extensive – and costly – changes for production and it was therefore modified in-house by Gunnar Sjögren.

Introduced at the New York International Auto Show in April 1970, the Sonett III carried over the 1.5-litre V4 engine and fibreglass body construction of the previous model. It achieved a very creditable Cd figure of just 0.31, thanks to its Kamm tail and low front with pop-up headlamps. Legislation in the US, the car's biggest market, dictated, however, that additional spot lamps be fitted in the front grille. Access to the luggage compartment was now through a more convenient hinged rear window. A roll bar, tinted glass and improved seats were all fitted as standard.

The Sonett III had a sportier appearance

TRANSMISSION: Final drive ratio: 4.67:1.
WHEELS & TYRES: 4.5J x 15in, 155 SR 15 radial-ply tyres.
SUSPENSION: Front: anti-roll bar added.
DIMENSIONS: Length: 3.78m (149in).
KERB WEIGHT: 815kg (1797lb).
PERFORMANCE FIGURES: Top speed: 94mph (151km/h); 0-60mph (96km/h): 12.3sec; **overall fuel consumption:** 31-35mpg (8-9 litres/100km).

One of the very first Sonett IIIs in 1970, showing off its pop-up headlamps and standard-fit chrome hubcaps.

This illustration of a 1971 Sonett III depicts the original design of optional alloy wheel, made by Tunaverken in Sweden.

than the V4, with stripes often applied to each door, and alloy wheels available as an option, in place of the standard steel wheels with chrome hubcaps. Inside, there was a new dashboard with three round dials, and a floor-mounted gear change. The standard upholstery was a very 1970s orange-brown corduroy, but in the US, a luxury model was available with brown leather upholstery and dealer-fitted 'Coolair' air-conditioning.

From 1971, the capacity of the V4 engine was increased to 1.7 litres, to meet US emissions regulations. The following year, the car gained a new matt black grille and all-silver alloy wheels in the same style as those fitted to the 99 EMS.

1973 saw the biggest change to the Sonett III's appearance, with the arrival of the unwieldy impact-absorbent bumpers now required in the US. There were minor trim changes inside and new colour choices. For the 1974 model year, headlamp wipers became available and the alloy wheels now had contrasting black sections.

The interior of a Sonett III from 1972.

The Sonett III's styling was much cleaner before the imposition of safety bumpers.

A car from the final year of production, with the now mandatory impact-absorbent bumpers and silver-and-black alloy wheels.

The launch of the Sonett III had boosted its appeal, and it was by far the most successful version of the Sonett. Sales of all sports cars suffered, however, in the wake of the 1973/74 oil crisis and production of the Sonett III came to an end in 1974.

NUMBER PRODUCED: 8348.
PRICE AT LAUNCH (US): $4000.
ENGINE: 1498cc V4 petrol (1698cc from 1971), as fitted to 95 and 96 V4 (see page 37).
TRANSMISSION: Front-wheel drive, four-speed all-synchromesh manual gearbox with floor change and freewheel. **Final drive ratio:** 4.67:1.
BRAKES: Front: discs; **rear:** drums. Diagonal dual-circuit hydraulic system.
WHEELS & TYRES: 4.5J x 15in, Pirelli Cinturato 155 SR 15 radial-ply tyres (165 SR 15 from 1972).
SUSPENSION: Front: independent, with double wishbones, coil springs, telescopic shock absorbers and anti-roll bar; **rear:** rigid U-shaped axle, coil springs and telescopic shock absorbers.
STEERING: rack and pinion; **turning circle:** 9.4m (31ft).
ELECTRICAL SYSTEM: 12-volt; **battery capacity:** 33Ah.
DIMENSIONS: Length: 3.90m (154in), 4.06m (160in) with safety bumpers; **width:** 1.50m (59in); **height:** 1.19m (47in); **wheelbase:** 2.15m (85in); **track (front & rear):** 1.23m (48in); **fuel tank:** 60 litres (13.2gal).
KERB WEIGHT: 820kg (1808lb).
PERFORMANCE FIGURES: Top speed: 106mph (170km/h); **0-62mph (100km/h):** 12sec; **overall fuel consumption:** 31mpg (9 litres/100km).
COLOURS (1974): Baja Red, Burnt Orange, Mellow Yellow, True Blue, Emerald Green.

SAAB 99 AND 90

Saab 99

By 1964, 15 years after the first examples of the 92 had been built, Saab was producing more than 40,000 cars each year. More than 40 per cent of these were sold outside Sweden, particularly in the US and UK. But the 96 was already an ageing design and Saab needed a new, more upmarket model that would both appeal to 96 owners looking to trade up, and win new customers for the brand.

The decision to develop that car – known internally as 'Gudmund' or 'Project F' – was approved by Saab's board on Gudmund's Day (2 April) in 1964. The underlying design principles for the new model had already been established, however, two years earlier, when the company's engineers and designers had begun work on the project. Like all Saabs, the new car would be aerodynamically efficient, safe and solidly built. Front-wheel drive was a given and it would offer better performance and more space inside than the 96. As early as 1964, a three-door estate model was also considered.

Despite the growth the company had enjoyed, Saab did not have the resources to develop a completely new engine of its own, something that would become a leitmotiv in the company's history. In 1962, Saab therefore began discussions with the British engineering consultancy Ricardo. It soon transpired that the British car maker Triumph was also looking to develop an engine with similar overall characteristics. In February

Installing the engine in the body of the 99.

1965, the two manufacturers signed an agreement for Triumph to supply Saab with 1.5- and then 1.7-litre four-cylinder engines; these would initially be built by Triumph at Coventry in the UK.

The new engine was a four-stroke unit with a single overhead camshaft. Triumph used 1854cc and 1998cc versions of this in its rear-wheel drive Dolomite saloon, built from 1972-1980. The engine was tilted over at 45 degrees, as Triumph also planned to develop a V8 engine for its future Stag sports car, using the same cylinder head design.

Named the 99 – the next available number in Saab's traditional sequence of model names – the new car would be the last car styled by Sixten Sason before his premature death. It was initially offered solely as a conventional two-door saloon, with a wider track than the 96 to make it a genuine five-seater. At 0.37, the drag coefficient was slightly worse than

The original two-door 99 from 1969, as depicted by Rony Lutz.

The two-litre engine in the Triumph Dolomite Sprint had a 16-valve head.

the 96, but remained far ahead of many competitors at a time when values of 0.45 were typical. It had a distinctive concave rear and a front-hinged clamshell bonnet, which would become recurring elements in Saab's design language.

The doors completely covered the sills, preventing users from getting their clothes dirty in wet or snowy conditions. The headlamps were rectangular units, like those adopted by the 95 and 96 in 1969, except in the US, where four round headlamps were fitted instead, to comply with local legislation. All the brightwork was made from high-quality stainless steel.

Safety was a key part of the design brief for the 99, which had energy-absorbing 'crumple zones' at front and rear, the strongest ever windscreen pillars fitted to a production car and a collapsible steering column. Saab attached just as much importance to active as passive safety, and the new car had a sophisticated suspension setup: this ensured good handling and was clearly capable of coping with more power.

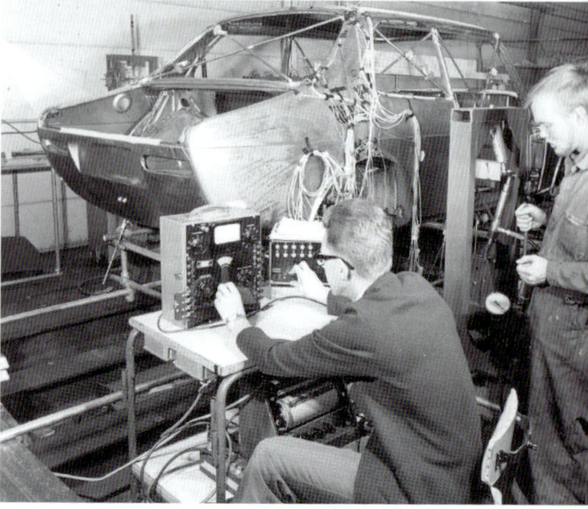

Saab's engineers evaluating the torsional rigidity of the 99's bodyshell in 1966.

Inside the car, the original dashboard was a simple three-dial affair, finished in black and clearly positioned in front of the driver. The instrument lighting was green, to make the gauges more comfortable for the driver to read at night, a feature that would continue until the final 9-4X and 9-5 models in 2011. As in the 96, the rear seat could be folded down to increase luggage capacity.

The first four prototypes of the 99 were nicknamed 'Paddan' ('toad'), due to their

Before and after ... After the car was dropped on its roof, the windscreen pillars remained impressively intact.

One of Saab's first marketing photographs of the 99.

incongruous appearance: Saab cut some dark green 96s down the middle and widened them by about 20cm (8in) to install the new drivetrain. By 1967, Saab had moved on to testing cars with the definitive body, but cunningly badged them 'Daihatsu' (a marque then unknown in Europe) to deflect attention from them.

The first engine that Saab tested from Triumph was a 1.3-litre version of the single overhead-cam slant-four, but it produced a meagre 55bhp (DIN). Even the 1.5-litre version offered only 68bhp, which was still too close to the 65bhp developed by the (lighter) 96 V4 model. Saab therefore decided to begin production of the 99 with the more powerful 1.7-litre engine producing 80bhp (DIN). This was mated to a four-speed manual gearbox with a conventional floor change, rather than the increasingly outdated column change fitted to the 96.

Production of a pilot series of 50 cars began in June 1967. In November that year, the 99 was officially presented to Saab's dealers and the press, and sales began in August 1968 (for the 1969 model year). For the North American market, the new model was introduced at the New York International Auto Show in April 1969.

The new car met with a somewhat mixed reception. It was as expensive as a Volvo, but didn't look as big, while the press criticised its lack of performance in comparison to rivals such as the BMW 2002 or Alfa Romeo Giulia. There were worries too about the potential reliability of its British engine. These concerns were offset, however, by the new model's high build quality, comfort and safety features. Compared with its German rivals, it was also well equipped as standard.

During the 16 years it was in production, the 99 won over more customers and reviewers thanks to Saab's process of continuous improvement and the many innovations it introduced.

1970 saw the first two major changes to the 99, with the introduction of a four-door saloon version (the CM4) and the launch of the 99 EA. The 99 E Automatic had a three-speed Borg-Warner Type 35 automatic transmission, while the 1.7-litre engine was equipped – for the first time on a Saab – with Bosch electronic fuel-injection in place of the standard model's single Zenith-Stromberg carburettor. The maximum torque remained unchanged, but power increased from 80bhp to 87bhp (DIN).

In 1971, a larger 1854cc unit (the same displacement as the version of the engine fitted to the Triumph Dolomite) was introduced, initially alongside the existing 1709cc engine. The new engine developed 86bhp (DIN) with a carburettor or 95bhp with fuel-injection; the 1.7-litre version was now only available with manual transmission and a carburettor, while the 1.85-litre unit could be specified with a carburettor or fuel-injection in combination

An early four-door 99, with steel bumpers.

with manual transmission, but only with fuel-injection in automatic form. During 1971, Saab's familiar freewheel device was quietly dropped.

More changes were introduced in 1971: there was a new design of dashboard, with three deeply recessed dials and a wood-effect trim strip at the bottom, and the 99 became the first car to be fitted with headlamp wipers as standard.

For the 1972 model year, Saab continued to innovate, introducing an electrically-heated driver's seat, which was activated automatically. Side-impact bars (another Saab first) and impact-absorbent bumpers were fitted, the latter necessitating a change to the position of the front indicators. The original 1.7-litre engine was discontinued and Saab brought its engine development and production fully in-house, at its new plant

Saab's engineers Kåre Rumar and Rolf Mellde next to the 99 with its pioneering headlamp wipers.

This cutaway drawing from 1974 shows the operation of Saab's heated driver's seat.

at Södertälje. Although Triumph would fit a 16-valve 1998cc version of its engine to the Dolomite Sprint, it never went down the path of fuel-injection or turbocharging.

The first model to have a Swedish-built engine was the all-new 99 EMS, launched in January 1972. Positioned as a sporty and well-equipped two-door model to compete with cars like the Volvo 142S or BMW 2002, its engine was bored out to 1985cc and was fitted with Bosch Jetronic fuel-injection to produce 110bhp (DIN). The standard kit included halogen headlamps, a rev counter and leather steering wheel. Externally, it had distinctive 'soccer ball' alloy wheels, which were also fitted to the Sonett III. The first cars were finished in Copper Coral metallic, followed by Silver metallic for 1974. An appealing model, it paved the way for the 99 Turbo.

At the end of 1972, a carburettor-fed version of the 2.0-litre engine became available on the regular two- and four-door models. A basic X7 two-door version was added to the range, mainly for the Nordic markets: this was powered by an 88bhp (DIN) version of the 1.85-litre engine and had simpler trim and equipment, with plain steel bumpers, more basic wheeltrims and rubber mats; it also made do without the heated driver's seat. Otherwise, for 1973, most cars sold worldwide had the 2.0-litre engine, and in the US all cars had fuel-injection.

This four-door 99 from 1972 has the new impact-absorbent bumpers.

The bumpers would return to their original shape after an impact at low speeds.

A 1974 99 EMS, in Silver with a black vinyl roof.

Stig Blomqvist and Hans Sylvan in their 99 EMS on the 1977 Swedish Rally.

A 1974 99 L four-door, with the single-carburettor two-litre engine.

In August 1973, Saab launched the 99 Combi Coupé (known as the 99 WagonBack Sedan in the US), inaugurating a body style that would be associated with the marque for nearly 30 years. Designed by Björn Envall, it was a three-door hatchback with a sweeping rear section and huge lift-up tailgate, which gave access to an enormous load area. From May 1975, a van based on the Combi Coupé was added to the range, primarily as a tax-break model in markets such as Denmark and Belgium.

All 1974 model year cars had new high-backed front seats with integrated head restraints, and inertia-reel rear seatbelts, while the EMS now came with a black vinyl roof as standard. For the first time on any Saab, power-assisted steering was offered as an option on four-door 99s with automatic transmission, a combination particularly appreciated in North America.

For 1975, the 2.0-litre engine was standardised across the range and three different versions were available: with a single carburettor, producing 100bhp (DIN) in L trim; with twin Zenith-Stromberg carburettors,

developing 108bhp as the GL Super; and finally with fuel-injection, now producing 118bhp.

At the Brussels Motor Show in January 1976, Saab added the luxurious new 99 GLE to the range. Based on the four-door saloon, it was powered by the 118bhp fuel-injected engine from the EMS, but with automatic transmission and power steering. The alloy wheels were similar in design to those on the EMS, but with gold rather than black accents. Standard equipment included a heated seat for the front passenger as well as the driver, rear seat headrests and centre armrest, velour upholstery and an electrically operated door mirror which could be adjusted from inside the car.

Two months later, at the 1976 Geneva Motor Show, Saab launched the five-door version of its Combi Coupé, initially available with the 108bhp twin-carburettor engine and a choice of manual or automatic transmission. A GLE five-door followed in 1978. Its distinctive 'opera' windows behind the rear doors proved controversial and Envall admitted it was not the most elegant design, but Saab's resources were limited. With other large five-door family hatchbacks such as the Rover SD1, Audi

Two views of the three-door Combi Coupé from 1974, in a very period shade of orange.

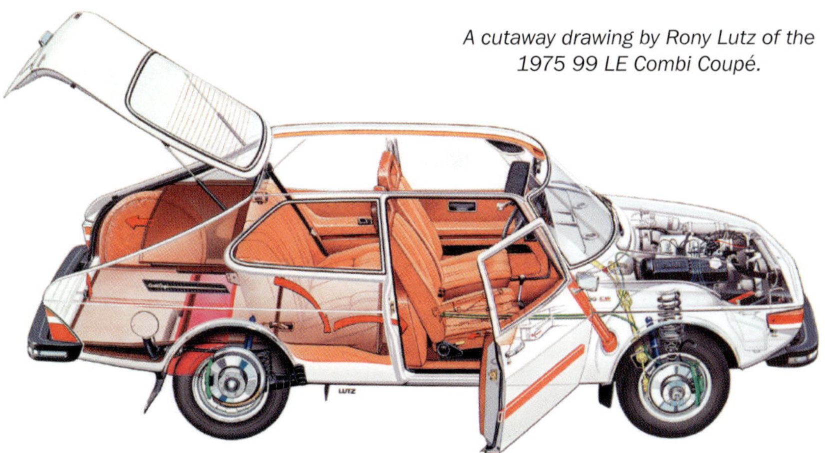

A cutaway drawing by Rony Lutz of the 1975 99 LE Combi Coupé.

Dyno-testing a US-market 99 with four round headlamps in 1977.

100 Avant and Renault 20/30 all entering the market, it was in any event a well-timed addition to the range.

The 99 GLE five-door served as the basis for one of Saab's more unusual models, the 99 Finlandia, introduced in 1977. The idea originated from a discussion between Finland's President, Urho Kekkonen, and Marcus Wallenberg, Saab's major shareholder. Kekkonen wanted a more discreet official car than the Cadillac he was then using, so Wallenberg had a special stretched 99 built for him by a Swedish coachbuilder. When the one-off car was revealed in the press, it was very favourably received, prompting Valmet to put the Finlandia into production at its Uusikaupunki plant.

Sold only in Finland, it was a stretched limousine model, initially with an extra 25cm (10in) let in to the wheelbase and an additional side window fitted between the front and rear doors. The design was subsequently slightly changed, with the increase in the wheelbase reduced to 20cm (8in) and each door slightly lengthened, so that the additional side window could be dispensed with. Saab's

The 99 Finlandia was based on the five-door GLE Combi Coupé.

Swedish management was not particularly enthusiastic about the Finlandia, but it had set a precedent and an extended-wheelbase version of the 900 was also produced.

The most exciting news of all in the 99's career came in September 1977, when the 99 Turbo was unveiled at the Frankfurt Motor Show, and this is described in the separate section below.

In 1979, however, the spotlight began to move away from the 99, as Saab launched the new 900. The 99 range was therefore simplified and the three- and five-door Combi Coupés were dropped in nearly all markets. Saab nonetheless continued to make minor improvements to the 99, and in 1980, the 99 was fitted with the same front seats as the 900, with height adjustment for the headrests. There were new side mouldings and black trim around the wheelarches. The range comprised the GL with the 100bhp single-carburettor engine, the GLS with twin carburettors, producing 108bhp, and in some markets (including the US) the GLi automatic, with fuel-injection. From July 1980, a four-door GLE saloon with manual transmission was offered in the UK.

Over the next couple of years, Saab continued to rationalise its range and the 99 inherited several features introduced on the 900. These included the rear seats from the 900 in 1981 and the uprated 'H'-series engines from the 1982 model year. Asbestos-free brake pads, introduced for 1983, were another Saab first. Various minor changes were also made to the cars' interior and exterior trim. For 1984, the 99's last year of production, electronic ignition was fitted to all 99 models.

99 (1.7 two-door)

NUMBER PRODUCED: 588,643 (all models, including Turbo).

PRICE (UK – 1969): £1295.

ENGINE: Four-cylinder in-line petrol, mounted longitudinally and canted over at 45 degrees, cast iron block and aluminium cylinder head, chain-driven single overhead camshaft, water-cooled with electric fan, single Zenith-Stromberg 175 CD carburettor. **Bore:** 83.5mm; **stroke:** 78mm; **capacity:** 1709cc. **Compression ratio:** 9.0:1; **maximum power:** 80bhp (DIN) at 5200rpm; **maximum torque:** 127Nm (94lb·ft) at 3000rpm.

TRANSMISSION: Front-wheel drive, four-speed all-synchromesh manual gearbox with floor change and integrated ignition lock in reverse gear. Freewheel until 1971. **Final drive ratio:** 4.22:1.

BRAKES: Discs at front and rear, with servo assistance. Diagonal dual-circuit hydraulic system.

WHEELS & TYRES: 4.5J x 15in, 155 SR 15 radial-ply tyres.

SUSPENSION: Front: independent with double wishbones, coil springs and telescopic shock absorbers; **rear:** rigid axle with Watts links, coil springs, Panhard rod and telescopic shock absorbers.

This cutaway drawing by Rony Lutz shows a four-door 99 from 1980.

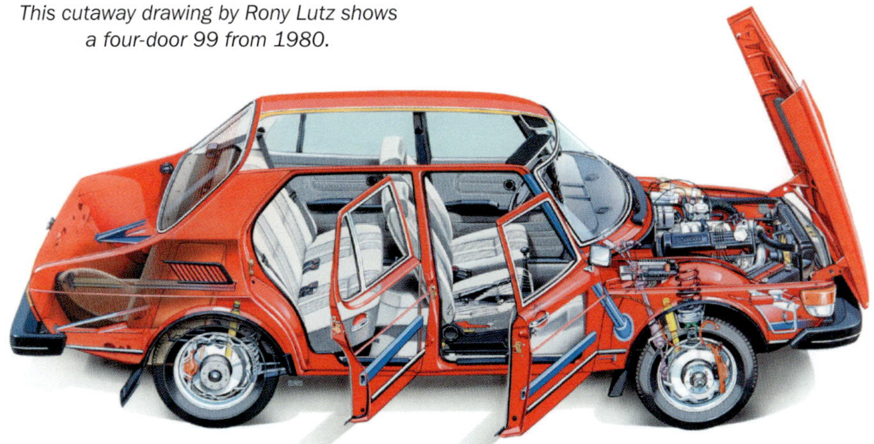

STEERING: Rack and pinion; **turning circle:** 10.4m (34ft).
ELECTRICAL SYSTEM: 12-volt; **battery capacity:** 60Ah.
DIMENSIONS: Length: 4.35m (171in); **width:** 1.68m (66in); **height:** 1.45m (57in); **wheelbase:** 2.47m (97in); **track:** front 1.39m (55in), rear 1.40m (55in).
KERB WEIGHT: 1035kg (2282lb).
CAPACITIES: Fuel: 48 litres (10.6gal); **boot:** 347 litres (12.2ft^3).
PERFORMANCE FIGURES: Top speed: 97mph (156km/h); **0-60mph (96km/h):** 15.2sec; **overall fuel consumption:** 24-28mpg (10-12 litres/100km).
COLOURS (1969): Red, white, blue, green, black, beige.

99 EA (1.85 four-door)
KEY DIFFERENCES

PRICE (UK – 1972): £1881.
ENGINE: Bosch electronic fuel-injection. **Bore:** 87mm; **stroke:** 78mm; **capacity:** 1854cc. **Compression ratio:** 9.0:1; **maximum power:** 97bhp (DIN) at 5200rpm; **maximum torque:** 142Nm (105lb·ft) at 3000rpm.
TRANSMISSION: Front-wheel drive, three-speed Borg-Warner Type 35 automatic transmission with floor change. **Final drive ratio:** 3.82:1.
KERB WEIGHT: 1118kg (2465lb).
PERFORMANCE FIGURES: Top speed: 94mph (151km/h); **0-60mph (96km/h):** 14.3sec; **overall fuel consumption:** 26mpg (11 litres/100km).
COLOURS (1972): Verona Green, Polar White, Mellanblå (Blue), Burgundy Red, Ambra (Yellow), Tyrol Green, Toreador Red.

99 EMS (two-door)
KEY DIFFERENCES

PRICE (UK – 1975): £2625.
ENGINE: Bosch Jetronic fuel-injection. **Bore:** 90mm; **stroke:** 78mm; **capacity:** 1985cc. **Compression ratio:** 8.7:1; **maximum power:** 110bhp (DIN) at 5500rpm (118bhp (DIN) from 1975); **maximum torque:** 167Nm (123lb·ft) at 3700rpm.
TRANSMISSION: Front-wheel drive, four-speed all-synchromesh manual gearbox with floor change and integrated ignition lock in reverse gear. **Final drive ratio:** 3.89:1.
WHEELS & TYRES: 4.5J x 15in alloy wheels, 165 SR 15 Michelin ZX radial-ply tyres.
STEERING: Rack and pinion; **turning circle:** 10.5m (34ft).
ELECTRICAL SYSTEM: 12-volt; **battery capacity:** 55Ah.
DIMENSIONS: Length: 4.42m (174in); **width:** 1.69m (67in); **height:** 1.44m (57in).
KERB WEIGHT: 1130kg (2491lb).
CAPACITIES: Fuel: 45 litres (9.9gal).
PERFORMANCE FIGURES: Top speed: 106mph (170km/h); **0-60mph (96km/h):** 10.3sec; **overall fuel consumption:** 24mpg (12 litres/100km).
COLOURS (1975): In UK, Silver metallic only.

99 Turbo

Saab wanted to offer a more powerful model above the EMS, but did not have the resources to develop a six-cylinder engine of its own. It therefore decided to develop a turbocharged version of the 99's existing 2.0-litre 'four', under the leadership of Per Gillbrand and with help from Scania's trucks division. As well as a turbocharger with a 'dump valve', this had strengthened internals and a revised camshaft. The company's aim was to increase the power of the engine, while making the car more civilised to drive than BMW's 2002 Turbo or Porsche's 930 Turbo, which were introduced not long before it.

With 145bhp (DIN), the 99's performance – and especially its mid-range acceleration – was transformed, leaving journalists and would-be customers who tried the car stunned. To handle the extra performance, the new model had front and rear spoilers, uprated Bilstein shock absorbers and Pirelli CN36 tyres, mounted on distinctive 'Inca' alloy wheels. The interior trim was similar to that of the 99 EMS, but with a turbo boost gauge on top of the dashboard and a standard sunroof and radio/cassette-player. All 99 Turbos were initially built with the three-door Combi Coupé body and most were finished in Jet Black with a dark red interior, although a few Cardinal Red and Pearlescent White cars were also produced.

Saab offered many special editions of its cars, often limited to particular markets. In the case of the 99 Turbo, these included a Turbo S with factory-installed water cooling, producing

A Jet Black 99 Turbo three-door, showing off its Inca alloys to good effect.

The interior of a 99 Turbo from 1978. Note the special upholstery and turbo boost gauge, mounted on top of the dash.

an extra 15-20bhp. In the UK, just 25 Cardinal Red 99 EMS five-doors were modified to receive the Turbo engine and other equipment.

Driven by Stig Blomqvist and Per Eklund, the 99 Turbo was Saab's last official works rally car, producing a heady 240bhp. In order to homologate the model for rallying, for which the stiffer, two-door body was preferred, Saab built 1000 two-door 99 Turbos, 600 of which came to the UK with right-hand drive. These were finished in red or black. Saab also produced a limited series of two-door 99 Turbos with simpler trim, finished for the most part in Marble White or Acacia Green. These were chiefly intended for sale by Saab-Valmet in Finland, but 300 cars also returned home to Sweden and a few found their way to other continental European markets.

The 99 and later 900 Turbo proved a massive success for Saab, and by 1983 the company had built more than 100,000 turbo-engined cars.

An Acacia Green 99 Turbo two-door.

Stig Blomqvist poses next to his 99 Turbo, equipped with four round headlamps and Minilite wheels.

99 Turbo (three-door)

PRICE (UK – 1978): £7850.
ENGINE: Four-cylinder in-line petrol, mounted longitudinally and canted over at 45 degrees, cast iron block and aluminium cylinder head, chain-driven single overhead camshaft and eight valves, water-cooled with electric fan. Bosch K-Jetronic fuel-injection, Garrett AiResearch turbocharger running 0.9bar (13psi) boost. **Bore:** 90mm; **stroke:** 78mm; **capacity:** 1985cc. **Compression ratio:** 7.2:1; **maximum power:** 145bhp (DIN) at 5000rpm (12bhp less for California); **maximum torque:** 236Nm (174lb·ft) at 3000rpm.
TRANSMISSION: Front-wheel drive, four-speed all-synchromesh manual gearbox with floor change and integrated ignition lock in reverse gear. **Final drive ratio:** 3.9:1.
BRAKES: Discs at front and rear, with servo assistance. Diagonal dual-circuit hydraulic system.
WHEELS & TYRES: 5.5J x 15in alloy wheels, 175/70 HR 15 Pirelli CN36 radial-ply tyres.
SUSPENSION: Front: independent with double wishbones, coil springs and Bilstein telescopic shock absorbers; **rear:** rigid axle with four-link location, coil springs, Panhard rod and Bilstein telescopic shock absorbers.

25 years after the launch of the 99 Turbo, Saab GB produced a commemorative 9-3 Turbo Anniversary Coupé.

STEERING: Rack and pinion; **turning circle:** 10.6m (35ft).
ELECTRICAL SYSTEM: 12-volt; **battery capacity:** 60Ah.
DIMENSIONS: **Length:** 4.53m (178in); **width:** 1.69m (67in); **height:** 1.44m (57in); **wheelbase:** 2.47m (97in); **track:** front 1.41m (55in), rear 1.43m (56in).
KERB WEIGHT: 1210kg (2668lb).
CAPACITIES: **Fuel:** 55 litres (12.1gal); **boot:** 350 litres (12.4ft^3), 1500 litres (53ft^3) with rear seats folded.
PERFORMANCE FIGURES: **Top speed:** 122mph (196km/h); **0-60mph (96km/h):** 8.9sec; **overall fuel consumption:** 21.4mpg (13.2 litres/100km).

Saab 90

As the 900 took Saab further upmarket, the company needed a cheaper new model lower down the range. The 96 had ceased production in 1980 and its intended successor, the Saab-Lancia 600, was a commercial disaster. Saab therefore took the unorthodox step of combining the front section of the 99 with the rear of the two-door 900 saloon. It was an inexpensive solution to develop, which had the added benefit of providing more space for rear-seat passengers and luggage. The name of the new model slotted into Saab's hierarchy at the time: 90 – 900 – 9000.

Introduced in 1984 for the 1985 model year, the 90 was only available with the basic 2.0-litre engine with a single carburettor, developing 100bhp (DIN). It was available with either a four- or five-speed manual gearbox; the five-speed versions were fitted with a front spoiler and lower-profile tyres, and could be specified with an optional sunroof. Compared with the last 99s, the 90 had a new, four-spoke safety steering wheel.

All 90s were built in Finland and the model had a relatively short career, from 1984-1987. During this time, there were relatively few changes to its specification. For 1986, side indicator repeaters were added and there were changes to the interior and exterior colours available. For the 1987 model year, the five-speed transmission became standard (although the four-speed was still available to special order) and the Zenith carburettor was modified for better cold starting. Minor

The Saab 90 seen from the side. Note the wheeltrims with a simple centre hubcap.

changes were made at the same time to the interior fittings. The last 90 came off the assembly line in Finland on 1 July 1987.

NUMBER PRODUCED: 25,378.
PRICE (UK – 1985): £6995.
ENGINE: Four-cylinder in-line petrol, mounted longitudinally and canted over at 45 degrees, cast iron block and aluminium cylinder head, chain-driven single overhead camshaft, water-cooled with electric fan, single Zenith carburettor. **Bore:** 90mm, **stroke:** 78mm, **capacity:** 1985cc. **Compression ratio:** 9.5:1, **maximum power:** 100bhp (DIN) at 5200rpm, **maximum torque:** 162Nm (120lb·ft) at 3500rpm.
TRANSMISSION: Front-wheel drive, four-speed all-synchromesh manual gearbox (five-speed optional) with floor change and integrated ignition lock in reverse gear.

De reeks Saab auto's is thans nog omvangrijker dan voorheen. De Saab 9000 Combi Sedan kan met de 16-kleppen injectie- of turbomotor geleverd worden. De vier verschillende motoren voor de Saab 900 kunnen in een Combi Coupé of Sedan worden geleverd. In de 900 serie bevindt zich ook een opwindende nieuwkomer – de Saab 900 Cabriolet. De tweedeurs Saab 90 wordt geleverd met carburatiemotor.

This Dutch-language brochure shows the 90 alongside the 900 Turbo, 900 Convertible and 9000.

BRAKES: Discs at front and rear, with servo assistance. Diagonal dual-circuit hydraulic system.
WHEELS & TYRES: 5.5J x 15in, 175/70 TR 15 radial-ply tyres.
SUSPENSION: Front: independent with double wishbones, coil springs and telescopic shock absorbers; **rear:** rigid axle with four-link location, coil springs, Panhard rod and telescopic shock absorbers.
STEERING: Rack and pinion, **turning circle:** 10.5m (34ft).
ELECTRICAL SYSTEM: 12-volt, battery **capacity:** 60Ah.
DIMENSIONS: Length: 4.58m (180in); **width:** 1.69m (67in); **height:** 1.43m (56in); **wheelbase:** 2.47m (97in); **track:** front 1.40m (55in), rear 1.43m (56in).
KERB WEIGHT: 1131kg (2493lb).
CAPACITIES: Fuel: 63l (13.9gal); **boot:** 617 litres (21.8ft^3), 1500 litres (53ft^3) with rear seats folded.
PERFORMANCE FIGURES: (All figures for five-speed manual) **Top speed:** 103mph (165km/h); **0-62mph (100km/h):** 14.0sec; **overall fuel consumption:** 26mpg (11 litres/100km).
COLOURS (1985): (solid) Cirrus White, Ivory, Azur Blue, Admiral Blue, Vermilion Red, Chestnut Brown, Black; (metallic) Silver, Rose Quartz, Platinum Blue, Pine Green, Cochineal Red, Slate Blue.

Bestuurdersplaats
De grote ronde instrumenten, die gemakkelijk af te lezen zijn, zijn keurig binnen uw gezichtsveld gegroepeerd zodat u uw ogen op de weg gericht kunt houden. De standaarduitrusting omvat een toerenteller met „economy" aanwijzing.

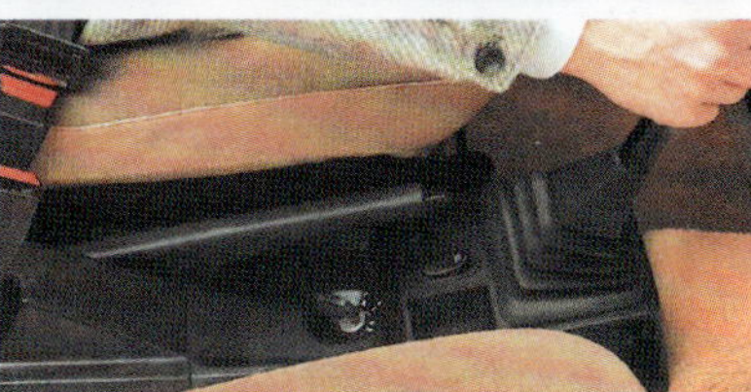

Middenconsole
De meeste bedieningsorganen voor het starten bevinden zich op de middenconsole tussen de voorstoelen.

Zuinigheid vormt een onderdeel van het rijplezier.

U kunt de Saab 90 zo hard laten rijden als het uitstekende weggedrag van de auto dit toestaat. De motor is ontworpen om er sportief mee te rijden, daar de kleppen direct worden bediend door de nokkenas en de motor een korte zuigerslag heeft.

Het genoegen van het bezitten van een Saab 90 heeft echter nog een andere dimensie, n.l. het lage brandstofverbruik. De 100 pk, tweeliter carburatiemotor is een uitstekende maar eenvoudige motor met weinig bewegende onderdelen. Dit draagt bij tot een goede brandstofzuinigheid en een buitengewoon lange levensduur.

De Saab 90 is uitgerust met een toerenteller met „economy" aanwijzing, die u in staat stelt zuinig met de brandstof om te gaan. Dankzij een aantal eigenschappen van de motor,

The dashboard of the 90 was carried over from the 99.

SAAB-LANCIA 600

When the 96 went out of production at the start of 1980, Saab was left with a major gap at the bottom of its product range. Both the 900 and later the 9000 took the brand successfully upmarket. Unfortunately, however, the company lacked the financial resources to develop a new entry-level model to compete with cars like the Volkswagen Golf in the fast-growing compact hatchback class.

Saab's main shareholder, the Wallenberg family, had long been friends with Gianni Agnelli, the president of Fiat. In 1976, Saab's dealers in Sweden began selling the Autobianchi A112, and the cooperation between the two groups subsequently expanded, leading not only to the Type Four project and the Saab 9000, but also the Saab-Lancia 600.

The Saab-Lancia 600 was, quite simply, a rebadged version of the Lancia Delta, a five-door hatchback designed by Giorgetto Giugiaro. Released in 1979, the Delta had front-wheel drive, fully independent suspension and a range of four-cylinder single-overhead cam engines. It was well appointed and positioned as a premium product, all of which augured well for the new Saab.

The range of cars sold by Saab dealers in Sweden in 1980.

The launch brochure for the 600, celebrating the election of the Lancia Delta as European Car of the Year.

Launched in 1980, the Saab-Lancia 600 had few changes from Lancia's Delta 1500. To cope with the severe conditions in Scandinavia, Saab fitted its own heater, an electrically-heated driver's seat and headlamp wipers. It also modified the rustproofing treatment of the cars, although they still rusted badly.

The 600 was sold only in the Nordic markets, with Volvo's 345 its main local rival. Two versions were initially offered: the GLS and the better-equipped GLE. The GLE had alloy wheels, a rev counter and a digital clock, but was dropped after only a year.

Unfortunately for Saab, sales of the 600 never took off , but it took until 1987 to clear the existing inventory. It was a victim of its high prices (a two-door Saab 99 GL cost only 1100SEK more than the 600 GLS), inadequate heating and poor rust protection.

NUMBER PRODUCED: 6419.
PRICE AT LAUNCH (SWEDEN): 45,500SEK
ENGINE: Transversely-mounted in-line four-cylinder petrol, inclined 20 degrees forwards, single overhead camshaft, water-cooled with electric fan, Weber twin-choke carburettor. **Bore:** 86.4mm; **stroke:** 63.9mm; **capacity:**

ROSTSKYDD FÖR RUSKVÄDER OCH NORDISK VARGAVINTER.

Genom ett ingående samarbete mellan Saab och Lancia har rostskyddet utvecklats till en nivå som helt motsvarar de krav bilägarna i de nordiska länderna kan ställa på sina bilar.

Svetsfogarna i bottenplattan exempelvis är som på övriga Saab-bilar uppdragna för att inte onödigtvis utsättas för fukt. De mest utsatta delarna av karossen är dessutom galvaniserade eller tillverkade av förzinkad plåt som är mycket motståndskraftig mot rost. Hela karossen »elektrodoppas» före lackeringen.

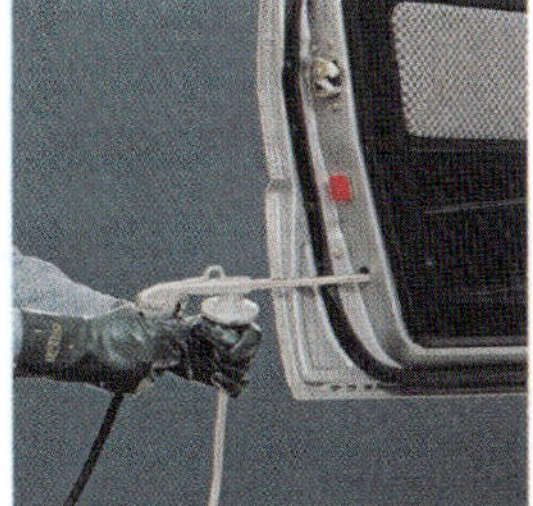

Varje bil specialbehandlas i en anläggning som f.ö. levererats av svenska Atlas Copco. Under högt tryck finfördelas en rostskyddande olja i alla hålrum. Hela underredet sprutas med PVC som ger ett starkt slitskydd. Och i främre hjulhusen monteras innerskärmar som fångar upp stensprut och hindrar att lacken skadas genom mekanisk nötning. Effektivare kan rostskyddet knappast bli.

Saab insisted that the 600 was thoroughly rustproofed.

1498cc. **Compression ratio:** 9.2:1; **maximum power:** 85bhp (DIN) at 5800rpm; **maximum torque:** 122Nm (90lb·ft) at 3500rpm.
TRANSMISSION: Front-wheel drive, five-speed all-synchromesh manual gearbox with floor change. **Final drive ratio:** 3.77:1.
BRAKES: Front: discs; **rear:** drums. Diagonal split circuit.
WHEELS & TYRES: 13in, 165/70 SR 13 radial-ply tyres.
SUSPENSION: Front & rear: independent with MacPherson struts coil springs, telescopic shock absorbers and anti-roll bar.
STEERING: Rack and pinion; **turning circle:** 11.0m (36ft).
ELECTRICAL SYSTEM: 12-volt; **battery capacity:** 55Ah.
DIMENSIONS: Length: 3.89m (153in); **width:** 1.62m (64in); **height:** 1.38m (54in); **wheelbase:** 2.48m (97in); **track (front & rear):** 1.40m (55in).
KERB WEIGHT: 1050kg (2315lb).
CAPACITIES: Fuel: 45 litres (9.9gal); 260 litres (9.2ft^3), 1000 litres (35.3ft^3) with rear seats folded.
PERFORMANCE FIGURES: Top speed: 103mph (165km/h); **0-62mph (100km/h):** 12.5sec; **overall fuel consumption:** 35mpg (8 litres/100km).

The GLS had a large analogue clock in place of the GLE's rev counter.

SAAB 900

After the 99 had been in production for more than a decade, its successor was eagerly awaited. By Saab's own admission, the company did not have the funds to develop an entirely new car, so the 900 was an extensively updated evolution of the 99, for which the company claimed more than 800 detailed improvements.

First unveiled in Trollhättan in May 1978, the 900 was presented at the Paris and Frankfurt Motor Shows that autumn, for launch as a 1979 model. Initially offered with three- or five-door bodies, it remained an aerodynamically efficient design, with a drag coefficient of just 0.34 for the basic version. From the A-pillars back, it was the same as the 99 Combi Coupé. The front of the car, however, was completely new, with a longer wheelbase and nose. The new frontal design not only refreshed the appearance of the 900, but improved its crash safety and provided more space under the bonnet for equipment such as power steering and air-conditioning. The company marketed it as "The new, longer Saab", a decidedly uninspiring slogan which, if the pun may be excused, sold the car short!

Among the many other changes to the new model were improved front suspension, a cabin pollen filter (a world first) and a new dashboard, whose design was claimed to be inspired by aviation, with large buttons that could be operated when wearing gloves. Large foam pads were installed in the doors to further improve side-impact protection.

The 900 continued to use the 1985cc

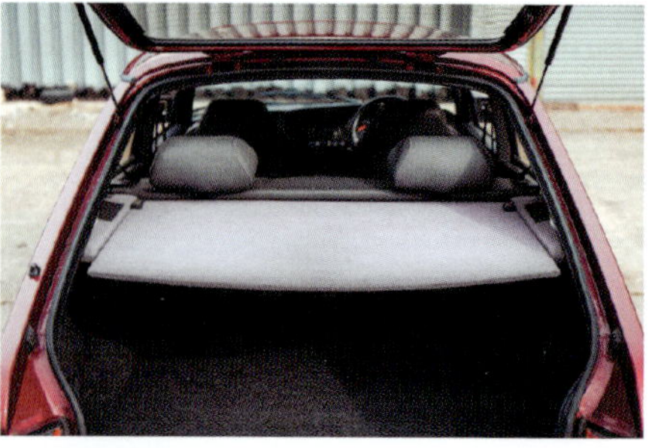

The 900 had the same cavernous luggage compartment as the 99 Combi Coupé.

The 900's dashboard – seen here in a 1986 Turbo 16 – was completely new.

The 1979 900 Turbo three-door seen in all its glory, thanks to Rony Lutz.

An entry-level three-door 900 GL from 1979.

'slant-four' engines from the 99. In Europe, the entry-level model in the range was the three-door GL with a single carburettor, followed by the twin-carburettor GLS (with three or five doors), which could be also be specified with automatic transmission, in which case power steering was fitted as standard. The next two models had the most powerful naturally aspirated engine, with fuel-injection: the sporty three-door EMS with a manual gearbox or the luxuriously appointed five-door GLE with standard automatic transmission and power steering. At the top of the 900 range were the two Turbo models, with either three or five doors. The EMS and Turbo had a different design of upholstery and a large rev counter (with a small inset clock).

Over the next 15 years, the 900 range developed enormously, as Saab increasingly aimed to compete with the premium German makes and moved further upmarket. Two- and four-door saloons were added, offering the same solid build quality, comfort and safety as the hatchbacks. But Saab also won new

At its launch, the five-door 900 GLE had these distinctive alloy wheels, supposedly inspired by the Bugatti 35.

The archetypal 900 Turbo three-door, in Black with 'Inca' alloy wheels.

customers for the brand with the stylish 900 Convertible, a first for the company and a body style that would continue for 25 years with the 900 NG and both generations of the 9-3.

The high-performance Turbo models became even more powerful from 1984, when Saab developed a 16-valve version of its 2.0-litre turbocharged engine for the 900 and 9000. Along the way, Saab continued to improve the specifications of all the 900 models and offered a huge number of special editions in each of its major markets. There is too little space here to describe each of these in detail, but there are separate sections below for the legendary Turbo and Convertible models.

The original 900, now often referred to as the 900 'Classic', was the last Saab to be developed before GM took a 50 per cent stake in the business and began to use the platform (and later engines and other major components too) from the Opel Vectra and other GM models. For many enthusiasts therefore, the original 900 was the last true Saab, and the Turbo and Convertible models now enjoy a cult following.

Saab's customary process of continuous improvement began for the 900 with the 1980 model year, when a five-speed manual gearbox became optional on the EMS and Turbo. There were also larger rear lights, a new grille and a new design of adjustable headrests, replacing the 'tombstone'-style seats carried over from the 99.

The big news in 1980, however, was the unveiling at the Geneva Motor Show of

Three generations of Saab convertibles, from the original 900 to the 9-3.

Two views of the 900 in production: in the paint shop and undergoing final assembly.

the four-door saloon (or Sedan), which went on sale that autumn. The spare wheel was relocated under the boot floor, freeing up extra space for luggage, while the rear seat backrest could be folded down, as on the 99.

In August 1980, the H-series engines were introduced, and were lighter and cheaper to build than the B-series engines they replaced. The letter 'H' stood for 'High compression', a development introduced to improve fuel consumption rather than performance.

For 1981, there were changes to the exterior trim, with larger mirrors and side mouldings. At the same time, the capacity of the fuel tank was increased from 58 litres (12.8gal) to 63 litres (13.9gal). The three-door EMS was discontinued and replaced by the GLi.

Saab revisited the concept of the 99 Finlandia with the luxurious 900 CD, built by Valmet in Finland. After producing a small number of five-door 900 Finlandias, Valmet

A 900 GLE four-door Sedan from 1983, with the later design of stainless steel wheels.

The four-door 900 Turbo, seen from the rear, now fitted with turbine-style alloy wheels.

applied the same treatment to the more elegant four-door saloon body to create the 900 CD. This had the turbocharged engine and automatic transmission, while the wheelbase and overall length of the body were increased by 20cm (8in) to provide more rear leg room. As with the second iteration of the 99 Finlandia, this was achieved by adding 10cm (4in) to the front and rear doors.

The cars' level of equipment steadily improved in 1982 and 1983. Power steering, already fitted to the GLE and Turbo, became standard or optional lower down the range, as did central locking. All five-speed manual cars now had a rev counter and econometer. Asbestos-free brake pads were fitted to all Saabs. For the 1983 model year, a five-door GLi with a fuel-injected 118bhp (DIN) engine replaced the GLE in some European markets.

For 1984, Saab launched two new versions of the 900: the two-door saloon (Sedan), available with naturally aspirated engines, and its new performance flagship, the Turbo 16, described in more detail below. New model names came in for the 1985 model

The badge says it all.

year: the GL moniker was dropped and the entry-level model was called simply the 900.

As 1986 arrived, Saab extended the use of 16-valve technology to its naturally aspirated engines, with the introduction in the US of the 900S, which signified the end of the basic 900 eight-valve engine. The 900 Turbo was now available with the two-door body, in addition to the three-, four- and five-door body styles. The 16-valve Turbo was also the only engine available when the 900 Convertible made its debut that year in North America (see separate section below). In the face of poor sales, however, the 900 CD was dropped.

By 1987, the 900 had been on sale for eight years and it was time for its first (and only) major facelift. The original 'flat nose' design was replaced by the so-called 'slant nose', with a sloping bonnet line and a new grille, headlamps and front bumpers.

In 1989, Saab introduced the 900S 16-valve models, with a naturally aspirated version of the Turbo 16 engine. Equipped with fuel-injection, this developed 133bhp (DIN), or 128bhp with a catalytic converter. All 900s with manual transmission benefitted from stronger gearboxes.

For the 1990 model year, the 16-valve engine in the 900S became available with a light-pressure turbo, another industry first: this developed 145bhp (DIN) and offered greater mid-range torque than the previous naturally aspirated unit. The capacity of the fuel tank on all models went up again, from 63 litres (13.9gal) to 68 litres (15.0 gal).

In 1991, a 2.1-litre version of the naturally aspirated version of the 16-valve

This UK-spec 900S Aero from 1993 has the later 'slant nose'.

engine was introduced, primarily for the US market, although some cars were also sold in continental Europe.

During the final years of the 900's career, ABS and catalytic converters became standard on all models in nearly all markets. The range was gradually simplified: the two-door saloon was dropped at the end of 1990, as was the Carlsson limited edition of the Turbo in the UK for 1993. Safety, however, remained a prime consideration for Saab until the end, with the headlamp wash/wipe improved in 1991 and a driver's airbag fitted in Europe (as well as the US) for 1993.

The last 900 'Classic' saloon came off the assembly lines on 26 March 1993, as Saab prepared to launch the new generation of 900; production of the Convertible meanwhile continued until February 1994. Together, the 99 and 900 had enjoyed a remarkable career lasting a quarter of a century.

Here's looking at you: the improved headlamp wash/wipe fitted from 1991.

900 GL/GLS three-door (1979/1981)

NUMBER PRODUCED: 908,810 (all models, including Turbo).

PRICES (UK – 1979): £5525 (GL)/£5775 (GLS).

ENGINE: Four-cylinder in-line petrol, mounted longitudinally and canted over at 45 degrees, cast iron block and aluminium cylinder head, five main bearings, chain-driven single overhead camshaft, water-cooled with electric fan, single Zenith 175 CD carburettor (GLS: twin Zenith 150 CD carburettors). **Bore:** 90mm; **stroke:** 78mm; **capacity:** 1985cc. **Compression ratio:** 9.2:1 (9.5:1 with H-series engine from 08/1980); **maximum power:** 100bhp (DIN) at 5200rpm (GLS: 108bhp (DIN) at 5200rpm); **maximum torque:** 151Nm (111lb·ft) at 3500rpm (GLS: 164Nm (121lb·ft) at 3300rpm).

TRANSMISSION: Front-wheel drive, four-speed all-synchromesh manual gearbox with floor change and integrated ignition lock in reverse gear. **Final drive ratio:** 3.89:1. Three-speed Borg-Warner automatic transmission optional on GLS.

BRAKES: Discs at front and rear, with servo assistance. Diagonal dual-circuit hydraulic system.

WHEELS & TYRES: 5J x 15in, 165 SR 15 radial-ply tyres.

SUSPENSION: Front: independent with double wishbones, coil springs and telescopic shock absorbers; **rear:** rigid axle with four trailing arms and Panhard rod, coil springs and telescopic shock absorbers.

STEERING: Rack and pinion; **turning circle:** 11.3m (37ft).
ELECTRICAL SYSTEM: 12-volt; **battery capacity:** 60Ah.
DIMENSIONS: **Length ('flat nose'):** 4.74m (187in); **width:** 1.69m (67in); **height:** 1.44m (57in); **wheelbase:** 2.52m (99in); **track:** front 1.42m (56in), rear 1.43m (56in).
KERB WEIGHT: 1155kg (2546lb).
CAPACITIES: **Fuel:** 58 litres (12.8gal); **boot:** 350 litres (12.4ft³), 1500 litres (53ft³) with rear seats folded.
PERFORMANCE FIGURES: **Top speed:** 100mph (161km/h); **0-60mph (96km/h):** 13.3sec; **overall fuel consumption:** 24.5mpg (11.5 litres/100km).
COLOURS – 1981: (solid) Cirrus White, Midnight Blue, Black, Alabaster Yellow, Cameo Beige, Terracotta, Dorado Brown; (metallic) Indigo Blue, Carmine Red, Pine Green.

900S 16-valve four-door (1989)
KEY DIFFERENCES

PRICE (UK – 1989): £14,195.
ENGINE: Dual overhead camshafts, four valves per cylinder, Bosch LH-Jetronic fuel-injection. **Compression ratio:** 10.1:1; **maximum power (non-catalysed version):** 133bhp (DIN) at 6000rpm; **maximum torque:** 173Nm (128lb·ft) at 3000rpm.
TRANSMISSION: Five-speed all-synchromesh manual gearbox. **Final drive ratio:** 3.67:1.
WHEELS & TYRES: 5.5J x 15in, 185/65 R 15 radial-ply tyres.
STEERING: Rack and pinion with power assistance; **turning circle:** 11.2m (37ft).
DIMENSIONS: **Length ('slant nose'):** 4.68m (184in); **height:** 1.42m (56in); **track:** front 1.43m (56in), rear 1.44m (57in).
KERB WEIGHT: 1270kg (2800lb).
CAPACITIES: **Fuel:** 63 litres (13.9gal); boot: 402 litres (14.2ft³).
PERFORMANCE FIGURES: **Top speed:** 115mph (186km/h); **0-62mph (100km/h):** 11.7sec; **overall fuel consumption:** 27.2mpg (10.4 litres/100km).
COLOURS: (solid) Cherry Red, Embassy Blue, Cirrus White, Garnet, Black; (metallic) Platinum Blue, Sandstone, Silver, Odoardo (in US: Edwardian Gray), Bronze, Malachite Green, Rose Quartz, Anthracite Grey, Carmosine Red.

900 Turbo

Following the success of the 99 Turbo, it was only natural that a Turbo model would sit at the top of the 900 range. The three-door continued with the Inca alloy wheels seen on the 99 Turbo, now shod with 195/60 Pirellis, whereas the five-door, which soon followed it, was fitted with Michelin's TRX tyres for extra comfort.

For 1981, a four-door Turbo saloon was added to the range and all Turbo models had a revised front spoiler. The five-speed

A 1980 900 Turbo three-door on the open road.

A four-door 900 Turbo from 1981.

Per Gillbrand poses with the APC system he developed for Saab's turbocharged engines.

The 900 Turbo's instrument cluster, with an 'APC' script added to the boost gauge.

manual gearbox was now standard on the Turbo, but the Borg-Warner Type 37 automatic transmission (a strengthened version of the Type 35) became an option.

For the 1982 model year, Saab introduced one of its most important technical innovations on the 900 Turbo: known as Automatic Performance Control (APC), this was a sophisticated electronic system which adjusted the turbo boost pressure for different grades of fuel (from 91-99 octane) and improved both performance and fuel consumption.

Saab's new performance flagship, the Turbo 16, was presented at the Brussels Motor Show in January 1984. By now, Saab was the biggest manufacturer of turbo-engined cars in the world and every third Saab sold was a Turbo model. For the first time, the 900 and 9000 Turbo 16 models had a 16-valve dual overhead-cam engine, equipped with an intercooler and Bosch LH-Jetronic fuel-injection. Power rose to 175bhp (DIN) for cars with a manual gearbox and 160bhp for automatics.

To top off the range, the Turbo 16 S, Aero or SPG (for Special Performance Group), the name depending on the market and model year, was based on the three-door 16-valve Turbo. It featured Saab's iconic three-spoke alloy wheels, stiffer suspension with anti-roll bars, and a bodykit, including a larger rear spoiler, developed by IAD in the UK.

The eight-valve Turbo continued in production, gaining a standard intercooler for the 1986 model year, increasing its maximum power to 155bhp (DIN), and also became available with the two-door body.

For 1988, the Garrett T3S turbocharger on the Turbo 16 was fitted with a water cooler for improved reliability. In the UK, Saab offered a Carlsson three-door special edition uprated to produce 185bhp (DIN). The following year, the eight-valve Turbo models were dropped.

The 1990 model year saw a change in supplier for the turbocharger, with a new Mitsubishi TE-05 unit promising improved response time with less lag. In some markets, a modified ECU boosted power further, to 185bhp, as for the Carlsson in the UK.

The 900 Turbo went out with a fanfare in 1993, with a number of special editions, including the Aero GT in France: 70 of these were built, all finished in Black with dark grey three-spoke alloy wheels and special upholstery in a mix of leather and woollen fabric.

Across the Channel, the 'Ruby' limited edition in the UK also had special upholstery; the bumpers were colour-coded in Ruby Red, but the Aero bodykit was not fitted. 150 examples were produced for the UK, along with a handful of left-hand drive cars for other European markets.

900 Turbo 16 S (Aero) three-door

NUMBER PRODUCED: 71,099 (all Turbo variants).

PRICE (UK – 1984): £14,490.

ENGINE: Four-cylinder in-line petrol, mounted longitudinally and canted over at 45 degrees, cast iron block and aluminium cylinder

A cutaway drawing by Rony Lutz of the B202L 16-valve Turbo engine.

A 16-valve Turbo engine in situ, just run in after 80,000 miles (129,000km).

Two marketing shots of the 900 Aero, from 1986 (silver) and 1992 (red).

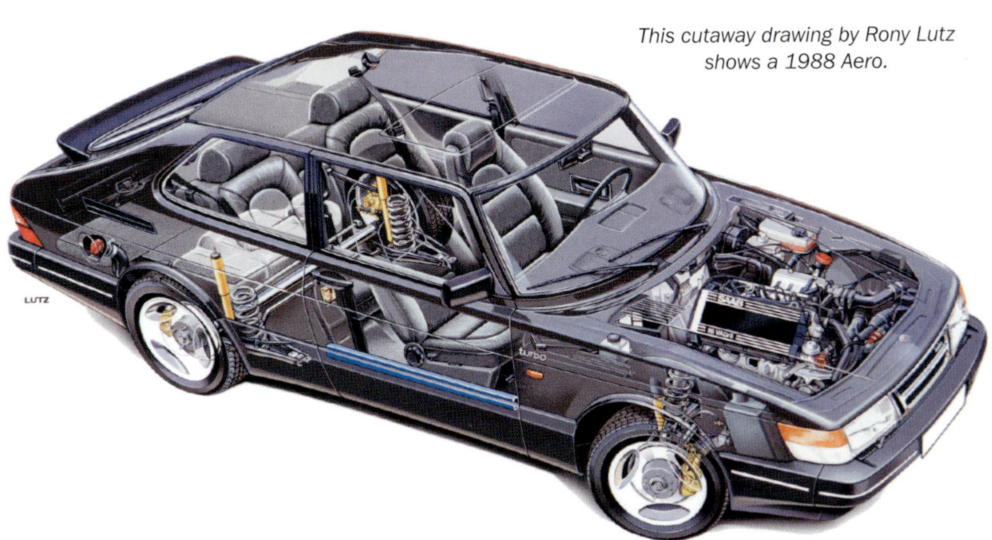

This cutaway drawing by Rony Lutz shows a 1988 Aero.

One of the run-out special editions from 1993, the French-market Aero GT.

One of the 150 'Ruby' special editions produced for the UK.

The lavish upholstery in the 'Ruby', with Bridge of Weir leather and woollen fabric by Ermenegildo Zegna.

head, five main bearings, dual overhead camshafts, four valves per cylinder, water-cooled with electric fan. Bosch LH-Jetronic fuel-injection, Garrett T3 turbocharger running 0.85bar (12.3psi) boost, with intercooler and Automatic Performance Control. **Bore:** 90mm; **stroke:** 78mm; **capacity:** 1985cc. **Compression ratio:** 9.0:1; **maximum power:** 175bhp (DIN) at 5300rpm; **maximum torque:** 273Nm (201lb·ft) at 3000rpm.

TRANSMISSION: Front-wheel drive, five-speed all-synchromesh manual gearbox with floor change and integrated ignition lock in reverse gear. **Final drive ratio:** 3.67:1.

BRAKES: Front: discs (ventilated from 1988); **rear:** discs, with servo assistance. Diagonal dual-circuit hydraulic system. ABS standard from 1989.

WHEELS & TYRES: 5.5J x 15in, 195/60 VR 15 radial-ply tyres.

SUSPENSION: Front: independent with double wishbones, coil springs and telescopic shock absorbers; **rear:** rigid axle with four trailing arms and Panhard rod, coil springs and telescopic shock absorbers. Anti-roll bars at front and rear.
STEERING: Rack and pinion with power assistance; **turning circle:** 11.2m (37ft).
ELECTRICAL SYSTEM: 12-volt; **battery capacity:** 60Ah.
DIMENSIONS: Length ('flat nose'): 4.74m (187in); **length ('slant nose'):** 4.69m (185in); **width:** 1.69m (67in); **height:** 1.42m (57in); **wheelbase:** 2.52m (99in); **track:** front 1.43m (56in), rear 1.44m (57in).
KERB WEIGHT: 1285-1310kg (2833-2888lb).
CAPACITIES: Fuel: 63 litres (13.9gal); **boot:** 408 litres (14.4ft^3), 1600 litres (56ft^3) with rear seats folded.
PERFORMANCE FIGURES: Top speed: 127mph (205km/h); **0-62mph (100km/h):** 8.7sec; **overall fuel consumption:** 21-24mpg (11.8-13.4 litres//100km).
COLOURS AT LAUNCH (1984): Black, Silver metallic.

900 Convertible

The impetus to develop the 900 Convertible was provided by Robert Sinclair, the President of Saab of America, who was keen to grow Saab's sales and move the brand further upmarket. Saab's directors – who had originally wanted Sinclair to take a lower-spec two-door saloon – were initially reluctant, but two convertible prototypes were nonetheless developed.

The first, designed in-house by Björn Envall, was based on the three-door body, while the second, produced by the American Sunroof Company (ASC), used the stiffer two-door saloon bodyshell. To overcome the need for an unsightly roll-over bar, it had stronger sills, a reinforced windscreen and sharply raked A-pillars. ASC's prototype was well received at the Frankfurt Motor Show in autumn 1983, and the proposal was signed

Open or closed, the 900 Convertible was all about enjoying the great outdoors.

Two 900 Turbo 16 convertibles, from 1986 (above) and 1987 (below).

off by the board the following spring, with production entrusted to Valmet in Finland.

The Convertible was launched in North America in 1986, powered by the 16-valve turbocharged engine, but only 379 'flat nose' cars were built before the entire 900 range was facelifted for 1987. Manual transmission was the only choice when the model went on sale in Europe in 1988, but in the US, there was also a catalysed version, downrated to 160bhp (DIN) to allow a three-speed automatic to be mated to it.

The Convertible was expensive but lavishly equipped, with leather upholstery, power steering, air-conditioning and heated seats as standard. The three-layer hood was electrically operated and had a heated glass rear screen, but took up a lot of room, making the 900 a four- rather than five-seater and reducing the size of the boot.

During its lifetime, the range of engines in the Convertible was gradually extended, with the addition of the 16-valve naturally aspirated unit and then the light-pressure turbo (LPT) engine. From 1991, the Aero bodykit also became available on the Convertible, with either the LPT or 'full-fat' turbos. The roster of safety kit also expanded, with ABS and a driver's airbag becoming standard equipment, first in North America and then in Europe.

With the car at a standstill, the hood could be raised or lowered in just 30 seconds.

One of the most sought-after 900 Convertibles today is the limited-edition Monte Carlo, which had very distinctive Monte Carlo Yellow paintwork and grey Buffalo leather upholstery. Just 300 of these were produced in 1991, although the colour remained an option (on the Convertible only) in 1992 and 1993.

900 Turbo 16 Convertible

NUMBER PRODUCED: 48,994.
PRICE AT LAUNCH (UK): £23,495.
MECHANICAL SPECIFICATION: See 900 Turbo 16 S (Aero) above.
DIMENSIONS: Length ('slant nose'): 4.68m (184in); **width:** 1.69m (67in); **height (hood raised):** 1.40m (55in); **wheelbase:** 2.52m (99in); **track:** front 1.43m (56in), rear 1.44m (57in).
KERB WEIGHT: 1335-1364kg (2943-3007lb).
CAPACITIES: Fuel: 63 litres (13.9gal); **boot:** 280 litres (9.9ft^3).
PERFORMANCE FIGURES: Top speed: 126mph (203km/h); **0-60mph (96km/h):** 7.5sec; **overall fuel consumption:** 23.4mpg (12.1 litres/100km).
COLOURS AT LAUNCH (1986): Cherry Red, Black, Cirrus White, Odoardo (in US: Edwardian Gray), Silver metallic.

This marketing photo from Saab GB in 1993 shows an entry-level 900 S Convertible with a relatively simple wheel design.

SAAB 900 NG AND 9-3 (FIRST GENERATION)

Saab 900 NG

The new-generation 900 (often referred to as the 900 NG) was the first Saab to be developed and launched after GM took a 50 per cent stake in the company at the end of 1989. Work on a successor to the original 900 had in fact begun in 1985, soon after the launch of the larger 9000, but none of the initial proposals came to fruition. The X67 project, based on the same platform as the 9000, was considered too big and too expensive to build, as was the later X102, while the X68B evolved into the 9000 CS.

Despite all the criticisms levelled at GM's involvement, Saab's engineers were aware of the savings in development costs and time to market that the American giant's resources offered them. No sooner had the ink dried on the GM deal than work began on the new 900 in January 1990, with the ambitious aim of having the first running prototypes in mid-1991 and pre-production cars ready by spring 1993.

GM wanted to position Saab as a premium European marque above Opel/Vauxhall and attract new buyers, but it was conscious of the need to preserve its brand identity and retain its existing customers.

The new 900 was based on the GM2900 platform used for the recently introduced Opel

Final assembly for some of the first 900s in 1993.

A studio shot of the 900 SE five-door from 1994.

Vectra A and the equivalent Vauxhall Cavalier. It actually used the reinforced floorpan of the Calibra coupé, which was built at Saab's Uusikaupunki factory in Finland from March 1992 to give its production teams experience of the new platform before the 900 NG came online. The rear suspension came from the Opel/Vauxhall Astra. It is easy to criticise Saab for this, but other premium manufacturers, including Audi and Jaguar, followed the same approach to platform or component sharing with greater or lesser success.

Geoff Wardle and Einar Hareide were responsible for the exterior design of the new model, working under the direction of Björn Envall. At launch in 1993, the new 900 was available only as a five-door hatchback, followed by three-door coupé and convertible models at the start of 1994. A conventional three-box saloon was never offered. The external dimensions were similar to the outgoing model, but with a longer wheelbase to provide more interior space. The bumpers were much better integrated into the overall shape and the clumsy 'opera' windows, first seen on the 99, were no more. Customer clinics confirmed that the new design was still recognisable as a Saab, and it retained the manufacturer's reputation for excellent aerodynamics, with a drag coefficient of just 0.30 for the base 2.0i models.

The 900 NG shared its platform with the Vauxhall Calibra.

Inside, the dashboard was completely new and had an integrated in-car entertainment system, as well as a simple trip computer, the Saab Information Display. The design was still inspired by aviation and the ignition key was mounted once again between the front seats. The 'Black Panel' feature was a notable innovation: at night, all the instruments except the speedometer could be dimmed, with additional information displayed only when required (eg, if the fuel level ran low).

The 900 NG had 60:40 split-folding rear seats, but Saab became the first car maker to fit three inertia-reel seatbelts in the rear of a hatchback. These were attached to a solid crossmember running across the car. This could be removed when the seats were folded down to provide uninterrupted access to the

This marketing shot shows the 900 SE five-door in a typical scenic setting.

The three-door coupé and convertible body styles soon followed the original five-door hatchback.

Below: The body of the new 900 was 55 per cent more rigid than the original model.

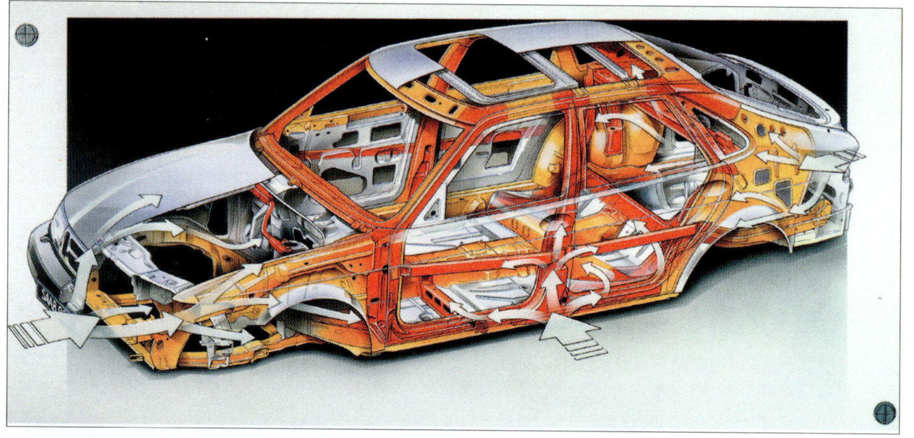

The overall design of the 900 NG's dashboard continued largely unchanged in the 9-3 models, such as this 1999 Convertible.

load area. The rear bench also featured an integrated child seat.

The four-cylinder petrol engines powering the new car were Saab's 16-valve dual overhead-cam units, but they were now installed transversely rather than longitudinally. In addition to the basic 2.0-litre naturally aspirated version, a more powerful 2.3-litre 'four' was available, with twin balancer shafts for smoother running. These were subsequently fitted to the 2.0-litre engine for 1995.

Early in 1994, Saab's hallmark 2.0-litre Turbo made its return as the performance flagship in the range, and in September that year, it became available with an entirely new semi-automatic transmission, known as 'Sensonic'. In essence, this was a clutchless manual transmission, with changes actuated when the driver started to move the gearlever. In January 1996, the 2.0 Turbo also became available with a conventional torque-converter automatic transmission.

For the first time on a production model, Saab offered a six-cylinder version of the 900, a key consideration for the US market. The engine was the four-cam 2.5 V6 built by Vauxhall at Ellesmere Port in the UK and fitted to the Opel/Vauxhall Vectra and Omega. Like the four-cylinder cars, it was available with a five-speed manual gearbox (until 1996)

The rear seat with three inertia-reel seatbelts.

The integrated child safety seat was another Saab innovation.

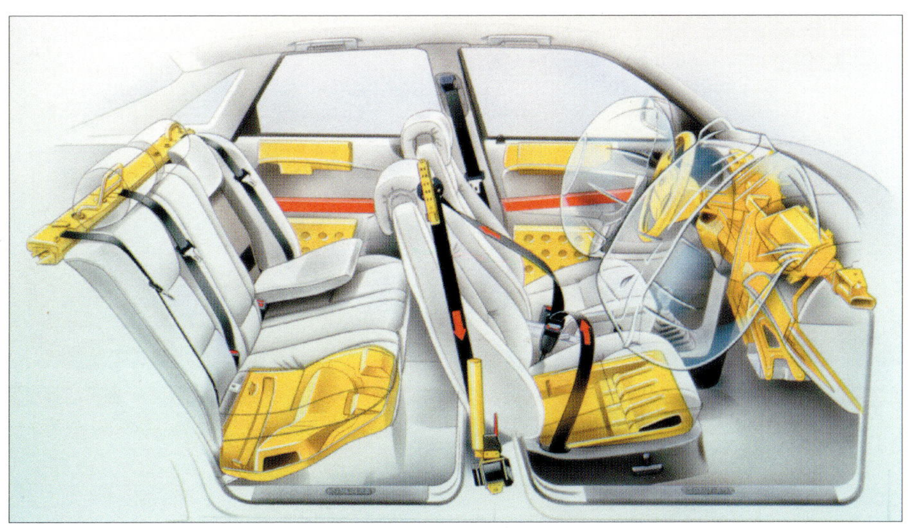

An overview of the interior safety systems in the 900 NG.

The engine bay of a 1995 2.0 Turbo, with the Sensonic control unit circled.

or a new four-speed automatic transmission supplied by Aisin-Warner, with three driving modes: Normal, Winter and Sport. Traction control was standard, another first for Saab. The V6 was dropped, however, for the 900's final model year (1998).

In keeping with Saab's premium positioning, nearly all the new 900s were well-equipped as standard, with the sole exception of the short-lived basic 900i. The exact specification varied by market, but the S trim level typically included ABS, electric windows and door mirrors, central locking, headlamp wash/wipe and a driver's airbag. The higher-level SE spec (the only trim offered with the V6 engine) generally added leather upholstery, automatic climate control, an uprated stereo system and cruise control.

Over the 900 NG's relatively short career, which ended with its replacement by the 9-3 in January 1998, Saab made various changes to the cars' trim and offered several special editions with extra equipment. These included the intermediate-spec XS in the UK and the Talladega models celebrating the 40 international speed records set by the 900 at the Talladega race track in 1996.

A cutaway view of the 900 SE V6.

Above: A 900 S 2.0 five-door, with plain wheel trims. Right: A 900 S 2.3 three-door coupé. Note the decorative trim panel above the number plate.

Both these three- and five-door SE models are fitted with Saab's handsome three-spoke alloy wheels.

These two cars illustrate some of the many alternative wheel designs available for the 900, as standard or optional equipment.

900 S 2.3i three/five-door

NUMBER PRODUCED: 273,578 (all models).
PRICES (UK – 1995): £18,495 (three- and five-door).
ENGINE: Four-cylinder in-line petrol, mounted transversely, cast iron block and aluminium cylinder head, water-cooled with electric fan, twin contra-rotating balancer shafts, dual overhead camshafts, four valves per cylinder, Bosch Motronic fuel-injection. **Bore:** 90mm; **stroke:** 90mm; **capacity:** 2290cc. **Compression ratio:** 10.5:1; **maximum power:** 150bhp (DIN) at 5700rpm; **maximum torque:** 210Nm (155lb·ft) at 4300rpm.
TRANSMISSION: Front-wheel drive, five-speed all-synchromesh manual gearbox with floor change and integrated ignition lock in reverse gear. **Final drive ratio:** 4.05:1. Four-speed automatic transmission optional.
BRAKES: Front: ventilated discs; **rear:** solid discs, with servo assistance. Diagonal dual-circuit hydraulic system, ABS.
WHEELS & TYRES: 6J x 15in, 185/65 or 195/60 R 15 radial-ply tyres.
SUSPENSION: Front: MacPherson struts and lower wishbones, coil springs and telescopic shock absorbers; **rear:** torsion beam axle, coil springs and telescopic shock absorbers. Anti-roll bars at front and rear.
STEERING: Rack and pinion with power assistance; **turning circle:** 10.5m (34ft).
ELECTRICAL SYSTEM: 12-volt; **battery capacity:** 60Ah.
DIMENSIONS: Length: 4.64m (183in); **width:** 1.71m (67in); **height:** 1.44m (57in); **wheelbase:** 2.60m (102in); **track:** front 1.45m (57in), rear 1.44m (57in).
KERB WEIGHT: 1325kg (2921lb).
CAPACITIES: Fuel: 68 litres (15.0gal); **boot:** 493 litres (17.4ft³), 1314 litres (46.4ft³) with rear seats folded.
PERFORMANCE FIGURES: Top speed: 125mph (201km/h); **0-60mph (96km/h):** 8.7sec; **overall fuel consumption:** 23.3mpg (12.1 litres/100km).
COLOURS (1995): (solid) Black, Cirrus White, Imola Red, Embassy Blue; (metallic) Citrin Beige, Silver, Ruby Red, Scarabe Green, Eucalyptus Green, Aubergine, Le Mans Blue.

900 SE 2.0 Turbo three/five-door KEY DIFFERENCES

PRICES (UK – 1995): £22,495 (three-door)/£22,995 (five-door).
ENGINE: Saab Trionic engine management system and fuel-injection, Garrett turbocharger running 0.95bar (13.8psi) boost, with intercooler and Automatic Performance Control. **Bore:** 90mm; **stroke:** 78mm; **capacity:** 1985cc. **Compression ratio:** 9.2:1; **maximum power:** 185bhp (DIN) at 5500rpm (with manual transmission); **maximum torque:** 263Nm (194lb·ft) at 2100rpm (manual).
TRANSMISSION: Five-speed manual gearbox, five-speed 'Sensonic' semi-automatic transmission (from 09/1994) or four-speed automatic transmission (from 01/1996).
WHEELS & TYRES: 6.5J x 16in, 205/50 ZR 16 radial-ply tyres.

Like all Saab convertibles, the 900 NG was exceptionally strong.

Open and closed views of a 900 Convertible in Silver metallic.

SUSPENSION: Gas-filled shock absorbers at front and rear.
KERB WEIGHT: 1365kg (3009lb).
PERFORMANCE FIGURES: Top speed: 135mph (217km/h); **0-60mph (96km/h):** 7.4sec; **overall fuel consumption:** 24.7mpg (11.4 litres/100km).

900 SE 2.5 V6 three/five-door
KEY DIFFERENCES

PRICES (UK – 1995): £22,295 (three-door)/£22,795 (five-door)
ENGINE: Transversely mounted 54-degree V6 petrol, four overhead camshafts (two per bank). **Bore:** 81.6mm; **stroke:** 79.6mm; **capacity:** 2498cc. **Compression ratio:** 10.8:1; **maximum power:** 170bhp (DIN) at 5900rpm; **maximum torque:** 227Nm (167lb·ft) at 4200rpm.
TRANSMISSION: Front-wheel drive, five-speed manual gearbox (until 1997) or four-speed automatic transmission. **Final drive ratio (automatic):** 2.65:1.
WHEELS & TYRES: 6J x 15in, 195/60 R 15 radial-ply tyres.
KERB WEIGHT: 1290-1425kg (2844-3142lb).
PERFORMANCE FIGURES: Top speed: 140mph (225km/h); **0-60mph (96km/h):** 8.7sec; **overall fuel consumption:** 24-28mpg (10-12 litres/100km).

900 Convertible

Production of the new 900 Convertible began at Valmet's plant in Finland in July 1994. In the UK, the range at launch comprised the 2.3i, 2.0 Turbo and 2.5 V6 models, all in SE spec, with leather seats and a three-layer hood supplied by ASC, with electro-hydraulic operation and a 40 per cent larger glass area than its predecessor.

KEY DIFFERENCES

PRICES (UK – 1995): £23,995 (2.3i); £28,195 (2.0 Turbo); £27,895 (V6).
DIMENSIONS: Height (with hood down): 1.44m (57in).
KERB WEIGHT: 1365-1465kg (3009-3230lb).
CAPACITIES: Boot: 285 litres (10.1ft^3)/354 litres (12.5ft^3) with hood down/up.

A 900 SE 2.0 Turbo convertible from 1997, in the striking shade of Monte Carlo Yellow.

The elegant flush-fitting hood can be seen here in Rony Lutz' drawing.

Saab 9-3 (first generation)

The successor to the 900 NG, the Saab 9-3 (pronounced 'nine-three') made its debut at the Detroit Auto Show in January 1998, alongside the all-new 9-5. In many ways, it was the car the 900 NG should always have been, and Saab claimed that 1100 improvements had been made to the new model.

Visually, the 9-3 was very similar to its predecessor, with the changes limited to a new grille and front bumper, and a relocated rear number plate. As before, it was available as a five-door hatchback, three-door coupé and convertible. Under the skin, however, the body structure had been strengthened, after the 900 NG suffered some embarrassingly poor results in the Euro NCAP crash tests. The mechanism for the hood fitted to the convertible was again developed by ASC, but was now operated entirely electrically.

Inside, the dashboard was carried over from the old model, but the climate control and audio systems (the latter now including a CD player, rather than the cassette deck fitted to the first 900 NGs) were updated. Saab's unique 'Black Panel' feature continued, but was renamed 'Night Panel'.

The revised frontal treatment of the 9-3.

For both the 9-3 and 9-5, Saab introduced its 'Active Head Restraints' (SAHR): these were designed to move the head restraints upwards and forwards in the event of a rear-end collision, so reducing whiplash injuries. Side airbags were also fitted as standard.

The suspension was much improved, with strengthened MacPherson struts and greater wheel travel to reduce understeer and provide a more dynamic drive. The most important mechanical changes to the 9-3, however, were to the powertrain. In Europe,

The rear number plate now occupied the place of the decorative tail panel on some versions of the 900 NG.

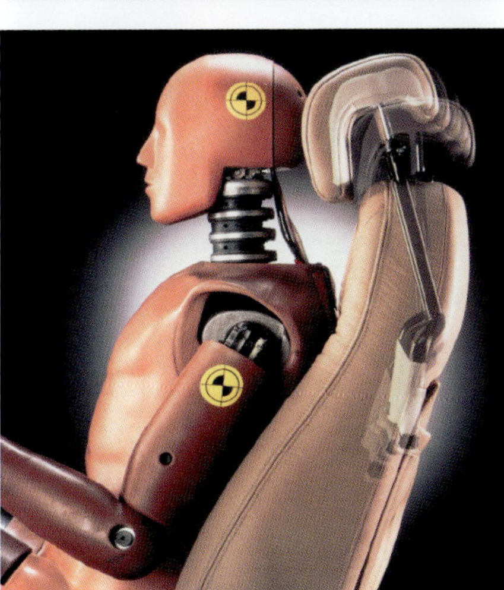

Left, top to bottom:
The interior of a 9-3 Aero Convertible from 2002.

A close-up view of the revised centre console. The dashboard of this UK car is finished in walnut veneer.

Saab's Active Head Restraint deployed.

the entry-level model was still equipped with the naturally aspirated 2.0i 16-valve unit. Immediately above this was the 2.3i engine, also naturally aspirated. This version was short-lived, however, as it was replaced for 1999 by the 2.0t Ecopower, when Saab reintroduced a light-pressure turbo, first seen on the original 900. Its maximum power output of 154bhp (DIN) was close to that of the 2.3 NA engine, but it offered greater torque lower down the rev range. The exact trim levels varied by market, engine and model year, but included base, S and SE models.

Surprisingly perhaps, the 2.5-litre V6 petrol engine was discontinued, and the sole engine available in the US was the 2.0 Turbo, now also billed as an Ecopower model. Initially, this produced 185bhp (DIN), like its predecessor, but for the 1999 model year, a 205bhp version of the engine was added. This was fitted to the Aero model, which also had a sports chassis, 16in alloy wheels, side skirts and a large rear spoiler, as well as leather sports seats. Saab dropped the Sensonic semi-automatic option, as sales of the 900 2.0 Turbo with this transmission had been disappointing.

There was more to come, however, as in September 1999, Saab launched the aptly named Viggen (Swedish for 'thunderbolt'), a new high-performance flagship for the range. This is described in more detail overleaf.

Less exciting, but essential for Saab's continued success in Europe, were the first

A five-door 9-3 SE from 2002.

Saab GB chose this Silver metallic Aero for the cover of its 2001 brochure.

diesel-engined models in the company's history. In May 1998, Saab launched the 9-3 2.2 TiD with a 2.2-litre diesel engine. This was developed by Steyr-Puch in Austria and manufactured by Opel, who fitted it soon afterwards to its Sintra MPV. It was a relatively advanced unit, with direct injection, 16 valves and twin balancer shafts for greater smoothness.

For 2000, the 205bhp Aero was fitted with traction control and the same spoilers previously fitted to the Viggen. In April that year, Saab celebrated 15 years since the introduction of its first convertible with the 9-3 SE Convertible Design Edition: available only in Silver, Steel Grey or Black, this had special dark grey leather with contrasting blue inserts and 17in five-spoke alloy wheels.

For many enthusiasts, the Viggen was the ultimate Saab.

The 9-3 SE Convertible Design Edition, introduced in 2000.

For the 2001 model year, the range of petrol engines available was simplified, with only the 2.0t, now producing 150bhp (DIN), and the 205bhp 2.0T remaining on sale. During the last two years in which the 9-3 was in production, Saab offered a number of special editions based on all three body styles, including the Polar and Sport editions, as well as tie-ups with Leica (customers received a Leica C11 camera with their car) and the French ski manufacturer Salomon.

Production of the first-generation 9-3 came to an end at Trollhättan on 8 May 2002, as Saab prepared to launch the second generation. Some five-door 2.0t Ecopower models, known as the 9-3 Combi Coupé, were built by Valmet in Finland until that autumn, for sale exclusively in the Nordic markets. Valmet also continued to manufacture the Convertible until April/May 2003.

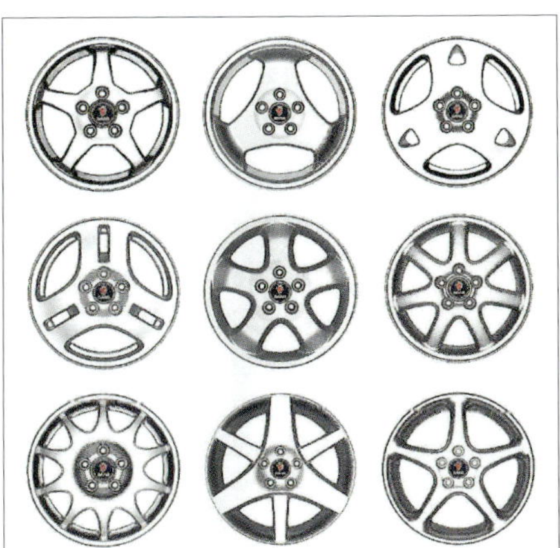

Saab offered a wealth of different alloy wheel designs on the 9-3.

9-3 2.0t SE three/five-door

NUMBER PRODUCED: 326,371 (all models, including Viggen).

PRICES (UK – 2000): £18,795 (three-door)/£19,295 (five-door).

ENGINE: Four-cylinder in-line petrol, mounted transversely, cast iron block and aluminium cylinder head, water-cooled with electric fan, twin contra-rotating balancer shafts, dual overhead camshafts, four valves per cylinder. Saab Trionic engine management system and fuel-injection, Garrett turbocharger with intercooler, running 0.4bar (5.8psi) boost. Three-way catalytic converter and Lambda sensor. **Bore:** 90mm; **stroke:** 78mm; **capacity:** 1985cc. **Compression ratio:** 9.2:1; **maximum power:** 150bhp (DIN) at 5500rpm; **maximum torque:** 240Nm (177lb·ft) at 1800rpm.

TRANSMISSION: Front-wheel drive, five-speed all-synchromesh manual gearbox with

Two views of a late-model 9-3 Aero Convertible.

floor change and integrated ignition lock in reverse gear. **Final drive ratio:** 4.05:1. Four-speed automatic transmission optional.
BRAKES: Front: ventilated discs; **rear:** solid discs, with servo assistance. Diagonal dual-circuit hydraulic system, ABS and EBD (Electronic Brake-force Distribution).
WHEELS & TYRES: 6J x 15in, 185/65 or 195/60 R 15 radial-ply tyres.
SUSPENSION: Front: MacPherson struts and lower wishbones, coil springs and gas-filled shock absorbers; **rear:** H-formed torsion beam axle, coil springs and gas-filled shock absorbers. Anti-roll bars at front and rear.
STEERING: Rack and pinion with power assistance; **turning circle:** 10.5m (34ft).
ELECTRICAL SYSTEM: 12-volt; **battery capacity:** 60Ah.
DIMENSIONS: Length: 4.63m (182in); **width:** 1.71m (67in); **height:** 1.43m (56in); **wheelbase:** 2.60m (102in); **track:** front 1.45m (57in), rear 1.44m (57in).
KERB WEIGHT: 1325kg (2921lb).
CAPACITIES: Fuel: 64 litres (14.1gal); **boot:** 494 litres (17.4ft³), 1314 litres (46.4ft³) with rear seats folded.

PERFORMANCE FIGURES: Top speed: 134mph (216km/h); **0-60mph (96km/h):** 8.0sec; **overall fuel consumption:** 31.7mpg (8.9 litres/100km).
COLOURS (2000): Black, Laser Red, Cirrus White, Silver, Midnight Blue, Steel Grey, Cosmic Blue, Sun Green.

9-3 2.2 TiD SE three/five-door KEY DIFFERENCES

PRICES (UK – 2000): £17,995 (three-door)/£18,495 (five-door).
ENGINE: Four-cylinder in-line turbodiesel, mounted transversely, cast iron block and aluminium cylinder head, water-cooled with electric fan, twin contra-rotating balancer shafts, single overhead camshaft, four valves per cylinder. Bosch Motronic engine management system and direct fuel-injection, Garrett turbocharger running 0.9bar (13psi) boost. **Bore:** 84.0mm; **stroke:** 98.0mm; **capacity:** 2171cc. **Compression ratio:** 19.5:1; **maximum pow**er: 115bhp (DIN) at 4300rpm (from 2000: 125bhp (DIN) at 4000rpm); **maximum torque:** 260Nm (192lb·ft) at 1900rpm (from 2000: 280Nm (206lb·ft) at 1500rpm).
TRANSMISSION: Five-speed all-synchromesh manual gearbox. **Final drive ratio:** 3.82:1.
ELECTRICAL SYSTEM: 12-volt; **battery capacity:** 85Ah.
KERB WEIGHT: 1394kg (3073lb).
CAPACITIES: Fuel: 68 litres (15.0gal).
PERFORMANCE FIGURES (115bhp): Top speed: 122mph (196km/h); **0-60mph (96km/h):** 10.0sec; **overall fuel consumption:** 35mpg (8 litres/100km).

9-3 Viggen

Named after the Saab 37 Viggen jet fighter and developed in conjunction with Tom Walkinshaw Racing in the UK, the 9-3 Viggen was powered by a 2.3-litre 'HOT' (High Output Turbo) engine, substantially uprated with a larger intercooler and 'Nimonic' valves. Running 1.0bar (14.5psi) boost, it developed 225bhp (DIN), increased to 230bhp for the 2000 model year. The Viggen also inaugurated Saab's new Trionic 7 engine management system; this was extended to the other petrol engines (now designated B205) for 2000, in the interest of reduced noise and lower fuel consumption.

Naturally, the chassis of the Viggen was uprated too, with 17in alloy wheels and much stiffer suspension. For 2001, a traction control system was fitted, but the Viggen never overcame a reputation for torque steer as its front-wheel drive chassis struggled to cope with so much power.

The Viggen was available with all three body styles, each featuring an exclusive bodykit and an even more imposing rear spoiler than on the Aero. A limited range of colours was offered, including the distinctive Lightning Blue often associated with the model. The interior was also specially equipped, with silver-grey carbon-fibre dashboard trim, heavily bolstered seats and two-tone leather upholstery with embossed Viggen delta logos.

From 2001, the Viggen was withdrawn from sale in Europe and the APAC markets, but remained on sale in North America. Altogether, only 4600 cars were built by Valmet in Finland.

9-3 Viggen KEY DIFFERENCES

NUMBER PRODUCED: 4600 (all body styles).
PRICES (UK – 2000): £31,000 (three/five-door)/£36,500 (Convertible).
ENGINE: Four-cylinder in-line petrol, mounted transversely, cast iron block and aluminium cylinder head, water-cooled with electric fan, twin contra-rotating balancer shafts, dual overhead camshafts, four valves per cylinder. Saab Trionic 7 engine management system and fuel-injection, Mitsubishi TD04 turbocharger running 1.0bar (14.5psi) boost, with intercooler. **Bore:** 90mm; **stroke:** 90mm; **capacity:** 2290cc. **Compression ratio:** 9.25:1; **maximum power:** 225bhp (DIN) at 5500rpm (230bhp from 2000); **maximum torque:** 342Nm (252lb·ft) from 2500–4000rpm (350Nm (258lb·ft) from 2000).
TRANSMISSION: Front-wheel drive, five-

A three-door Lightning Blue 9-3 Viggen next to its Viggen 37 namesake.

Rony Lutz produced this superb cutaway drawing of the Viggen.

Håkan Danielsson testing the airflow over a five-door Viggen.

The cockpit of a Viggen Convertible.

speed all-synchromesh manual gearbox. **Final drive ratio:** 4.05:1.
WHEELS & TYRES: 7.5J x 17in, 215/45 ZR 17 radial-ply tyres.
SUSPENSION: Uprated, with stiffened and lowered springs with revised spring rates, and firmer shock absorbers.
KERB WEIGHT: 1395kg (3075lb).
CAPACITIES: Fuel: 64 litres (14.1gal).
PERFORMANCE FIGURES: Top speed: 155mph (250km/h); **0-60mph (96km/h):** 6.5sec; **overall fuel consumption:** 29.4mpg (9.6 litres/100km).
COLOURS: Lightning Blue, Black, Silver, Steel Grey, Monte Carlo Yellow, Laser Red.

SAAB 9-3 (SECOND GENERATION)

The second-generation 9-3, Saab's first new car since GM had taken full control of the company, was truly a make-or-break model for the Swedish firm. First shown at the Detroit Auto Show in January 2002, production began in July that year. It was launched exclusively as a conventional four-door saloon, known as the SportSedan in the US or Sport Saloon in the UK. Saab's traditional three- and five-door hatchbacks were consigned to the history books, as GM sought to compete with the BMW 3-Series, Audi A4 and Mercedes C-Class, all of them three-box saloons.

The new 9-3 was built on the Epsilon platform used for the Vauxhall/Opel Vectra C, also introduced in 2002. The body had twice the torsional rigidity of the previous model, while the latest model was once again very efficient aerodynamically, with a Cd figure of just 0.28 in base trim.

A fact no doubt rued by GM's corporate accountants, the differences between the cars were, however, too great to allow GM to swap production of the various models between its various factories. Despite this, Saab's use of GM components went much further this time.

Saab's historic slant-four engines – which dated back 35 years, to the original 99 – were retired and replaced by a new series of GM

A 9-3 Vector saloon from 2003.

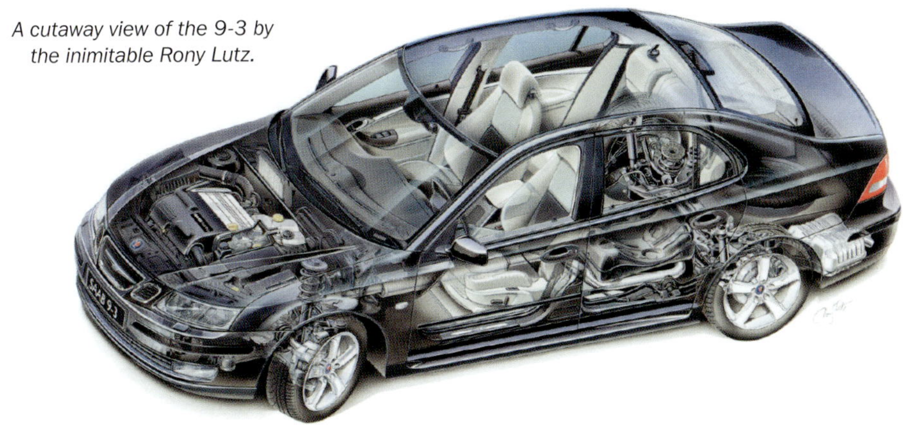

A cutaway view of the 9-3 by the inimitable Rony Lutz.

The lowered sport chassis of the Aero version made the most of the new suspension.

Ecotec in-line units. These were widely used in other GM models, including the Vectra, Astra and Zafira. For the 9-3, the 2.0-litre Ecotec engine was initially offered in three states of tune: the 150bhp (DIN) 1.8t (not sold in the US, and, despite its name, actually a two-litre engine), the 175bhp 2.0t – considered by many reviewers to be the sweet spot in the range – and the 210bhp 2.0T. The Trionic 8 engine management system and turbocharger installation, however, were specific to Saab. In Europe, the 125bhp (DIN) 2.2 TiD diesel engine was carried over from the first 9-3.

A five-speed manual gearbox was originally standard, with a six-speed 'box available on the 2.0T. A five-speed Aisin-Warner automatic transmission remained an option: this no longer had Sport or Winter modes, but allowed sequential manual changes.

The suspension of the new 9-3 was completely new, with a more sophisticated, fully independent multi-link setup at the rear. Saab's engineers aimed to create a sportier feel than the Vectra and went so far as to develop a special feature known as 'ReAxs', which applied a tiny amount of counter-steer at the rear to reduce understeer.

At launch, the 9-3 Sport Sedan/Sport Saloon was offered with four different trim levels, although not all engine/trim combinations were available, and there were differences between markets. The basic version was Linear, typically with 15in alloy wheels and cloth-trimmed seats; above this came the better-equipped Arc, with poplar veneer and leather upholstery, and sporty Vector trim levels. At the top of the range, the Aero – introduced at the Geneva Motor Show in March 2003 – had a lowered sport chassis

The interior of an Arc saloon, with poplar veneer inserts, leather upholstery and the Saab Infotainment system.

The Vector had a sportier look, with brushed metal-finish trim and part-leather, part-fabric seats.

with traction control and ESP, 17in alloy wheels, bodykit and sports seats.

Some reviewers criticised the quality of the interior fittings on the new model, but Saab kept some traditional features such as the 'Night Panel' dashboard illumination, joystick-operated air vents and the ignition key located between the seats (although this no longer locked the car in reverse gear). And for all the supposed synergies within GM, even the satnav was unique to Saab! All models retained a 60:40 split-folding rear seat to increase the luggage capacity.

Other standard or optional features promoted for their contribution to safety included Bluetooth technology for hands-free mobile phone use, a new generation of active head restraints (SAHR II), dual-stage front airbags, side and roof rail airbags, bi-xenon headlamps, an auto-dimming interior mirror and a rain sensor for the windscreen wipers.

For the 2004 model year, Saab introduced the Convertible, initially with the two more powerful petrol engines. The triple-layer roof had a magnesium frame and could now be operated in just 20 seconds. A new 'DynaCage' safety system incorporated a pair of pop-up roll-over bars behind the rear seats. The Convertible was built by Magna-Steyr in Austria until the end of 2009, when production moved to Trollhättan.

The dashboard of a 9-3 Aero, here fitted with the Saab Infotainment Plus system, including satellite navigation.

During 2004, Saab added a new entry-level petrol engine, the 122bhp (DIN) naturally-aspirated 1.8i. The following year, the 2.2 TiD diesel engine was replaced by a common-rail 1.9 TiD, sourced from Fiat. This was available (outside North America) as an 8-valve unit producing 120bhp (DIN) or as a 150bhp 16-valve. The latter was equipped with a diesel particulate filter and could be specified with a six-speed automatic transmission.

In March 2005, Saab launched the five-door SportWagon (also known as the Sport Combi or Sport-Hatch in some countries). For the 2006 model year, both this and the saloon could be specified with a new 2.8 V6

The side and roof rail airbags have been deployed in this offset front impact test.

Above: Inside the Convertible: the seatbelts were integrated into the seat frames.

Left: The Convertible with the hood raised and lowered.

This cutaway drawing shows the pop-up roll-over bars.

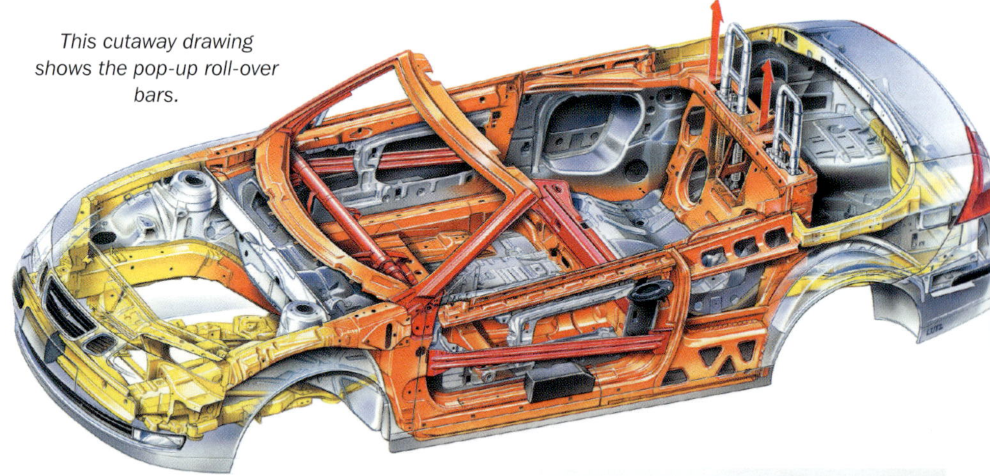

2005 ushered in a new generation of diesel engines.

Turbo engine, developed and built by Holden (part of GM) at Port Melbourne in Australia. It was a highly advanced all-aluminium unit, with four valves per cylinder and four chain-driven camshafts with electronically-controlled variable valve timing. It was a gloriously torquey engine and the manufacturer claimed it was the fastest Saab ever.

At the start of 2006, Saab celebrated 20 years since the first 900 Convertible with a special 20 Years Anniversary edition of the 9-3 Convertible: this had Electric Blue paintwork and matching blue inserts in its Parchment leather upholstery.

For the 2007 model year, Saab launched BioPower versions of the 1.8t and 2.0t, its

The author's 2006 2.8 V6 Turbo saloon, in Fusion Blue.

The SportWagon, here in Aero spec, had distinctive hockey stick-shaped taillamps.

The quad-cam 2.8 V6 engine was entirely new.

The overall styling of the 9-3 SportWagon was close to that of the 9-3 Sport-Hatch concept from 2003.

The striking 20 Years Anniversary Convertible.

first-ever engines able to run on bioethanol (E85) as well as regular petrol. At the same time, it comprehensively updated the design of the dashboard on all models. The controls for the heating, air-conditioning and stereo system were greatly simplified, and the Saab Information Display, previously located at the top of the dash, was integrated into the main instrument cluster.

This was just a prelude, however, to the major facelift for the 2008 model year. Restyled by the British designer Simon

A 1.8t BioPower saloon, introduced for 2007.

The new dashboard with the basic audio system and round dials to control the heating.

Padian, the updated 9-3 had new bumpers, new door panels (without the central trim strip on the saloons and estates) and Saab's traditional clamshell bonnet. Clear 'ice block' taillamps also gave the cars a more modern appearance. Power of the 2.8 V6 Turbo increased by a modest 5bhp. In the UK, the upgraded trim levels were now named Airflow (not available on the Convertible), Linear SE, Vector Sport and Aero.

In addition, two new models went on sale in 2008. The 1.9 TTiD – with Aero trim available for the first time on a diesel model – was fitted with a two-stage turbocharger and power went up to 180bhp (DIN), with an even more impressive torque figure of 400Nm (295lb·ft).

The second new model for 2008 was the four-wheel drive Turbo X, produced to celebrate 30 years of turbocharged Saabs. It was available in saloon or estate form, and with manual or automatic transmission (both with six speeds). Known as XWD, the fourth-generation Haldex system operated in conjunction with an electronically-controlled limited-slip differential (eLSD) and could

The new clamshell bonnet and more aggressive front-end design can be seen on this SportWagon.

The facelifted Convertible kept the side trim strips but had the new 'ice block' taillamps.

The TTiD boasted an impressive combination of performance and low emissions.

send up to 80 per cent of the power to the rear wheels. The turbo boost pressure of the 2.8-litre V6 was increased from 0.6bar (8.7psi) to 0.8bar (11.6psi). The brakes and suspension were also uprated, and special 18in or (outside North America) 19in alloy wheels were fitted. The Turbo X was built only for a single year, making it a sought-after model for collectors today.

From March 2008, four-wheel drive (XWD) became available on the 2.8 V6 Turbo Aero

The 9-3 Turbo X had a unique design of alloy wheel.

Inside, the Turbo X had heavily bolstered black leather sports seats.

"Ready for take-off." The Turbo X was the fastest-ever Saab car.

saloon and estate, which were also uprated to 280bhp (DIN) and 400Nm (295lb·ft) of torque. The 2.8 V6 Turbo Convertible continued to be available with front-wheel drive: it too developed 280bhp, but torque was limited to 370Nm (273lb·ft). The XWD option was extended to the 2.0 Turbo Aero saloon and estate a year later.

This coincided with the launch in March 2009 of the 9-3X. A stylish crossover closely based on the 9-3 SportWagon, it was similar in spirit to the Audi A4 Allroad or Volvo XC70. The 9-3X was available with either the 180bhp diesel or the 210bhp 2.0 Turbo, the latter in BioPower or petrol-only versions. Both models had distinctive exterior trim with roof rails, side sills, dark cladding around the wheelarches and aluminium-look front and rear skid plates, although these were really only for effect. Only the 2.0 Turbo, moreover, had the Haldex four-wheel drive system and self-levelling rear suspension.

During 2009, GM – which itself went into administration that year – put Saab up for sale, and at the end of a fraught process, it was bought by the Dutch supercar manufacturer Spyker in January 2010. This period saw several limited editions intended to boost the company's flagging sales. These included the 'Independence Edition' Convertible, of

The 9-3X was positioned as a 'lifestyle' model rather than as an out-and-out load-lugger.

The celebrations promised by the 'Independence Edition' Convertible sadly proved short-lived.

which Saab planned to build 366 examples to celebrate the first anniversary of its sale to Spyker. In the UK, this was sold only with the 180bhp TTiD engine and six-speed automatic transmission, finished in a unique Amber Orange metallic.

Alongside these special series, there were some final changes to both the diesel and petrol engines. For 2011, the single-turbo TiD engines were replaced by twin-turbo units, still with a choice of two or four valves per cylinder, each producing an extra 10bhp. An entry-level 163bhp (DIN) 2.0-litre BioPower engine was added, for both the 9-3 and 9-3X.

For what would be the final model year (2012), the 2.0 Turbo was uprated to produce 350Nm (258lb·ft) of torque, matching the original 2.8 V6 Turbo. The range of trim levels was simplified (in the UK, to SE and Aero; in France, to Griffin) and additional items such as electric folding mirrors or Bose surround sound became standard equipment. Various performance and appearance upgrades were also offered throughout the cars' lifetime by companies such as Abbott Racing in the UK, Hirsch in Switzerland or BSR and Maptun in Sweden.

Alas, Saab's financial problems only worsened during 2011, and in December it filed for bankruptcy and the production lines fell silent. 47 Convertibles were assembled from the remaining parts by the ANA dealer group in Sweden at the start of 2012, and NEVS briefly restarted production of the Saloon at the end of 2013, but the endeavour soon fizzled out.

One of the final Griffin-badged models sold in Europe.

Abbott Racing's R3 model was based on the 9-3 Vector and produced 220bhp.

9-3 2.0t Sport Saloon

NUMBER PRODUCED: 587,174 (all models, including 9-3X).
PRICE (UK – 2003): £21,595 (Vector).
ENGINE: Four-cylinder in-line petrol, mounted transversely, aluminium alloy cylinder head and block, water-cooled with electric fan, twin contra-rotating balancer shafts, dual overhead camshafts, four valves per cylinder, Saab Trionic 8 engine management with multi-point fuel-injection and Garrett GT20 turbocharger with intercooler, running 0.7bar (10.2psi) boost (Mitsubishi turbo from 2006). Three-way catalytic converter and Lambda sensor. **Bore:** 86mm; **stroke:** 86mm; **capacity:** 1998cc. **Compression ratio:** 9.5:1; **maximum power:** 175bhp (DIN) at 5500rpm; **maximum torque:** 264Nm (195lb·ft) at 2500rpm.
TRANSMISSION: Front-wheel drive, five-speed all-synchromesh manual gearbox with floor change. **Final drive ratio:** 3.51:1. Five-speed 'Sentronic' automatic transmission optional.
BRAKES: Front: ventilated discs; **rear:** solid discs. Diagonal dual-circuit hydraulic system. ABS, EBD and Brake Assist. TCS standard, ESP optional.
WHEELS & TYRES: 7.5J x 17in, 215/50 WR 17 radial-ply tyres.
SUSPENSION: Front: MacPherson struts with lower wishbones, coil springs and telescopic shock absorbers; **rear:** fully independent multi-link, with coil springs and telescopic shock absorbers. Anti-roll bars at front and rear.
STEERING: Rack and pinion with speed-sensitive power assistance, **turning circle:** 10.8m (35ft).
ELECTRICAL SYSTEM: 12-volt; **battery capacity:** 60Ah.
DIMENSIONS: Length: 4.64m (182in); **width:** 1.76m (69in); **height:** 1.47m (58in); **wheelbase:** 2.68m (105in); **track:** front 1.52m (60in), rear 1.51m (59in).
KERB WEIGHT: 1440kg (3175lb).
CAPACITIES: Fuel: 62 litres (13.6gal); **boot:** 425 litres (15.0ft^3). **Convertible boot capacity:** 235 litres (8.3ft^3)/352 litres (12.4ft^3) with hood down/up.
PERFORMANCE FIGURES: Top speed: 136mph (219km/h); **0-60mph (96km/h):** 7.7sec; **overall fuel consumption:** 26.4mpg (10.7 litres/100km).
COLOURS (2003): (solid) Polar White, Laser Red, Black, Dolphin Grey; (metallic) Silver, Steel Grey, Cosmic Blue, Midnight Blue, Merlot Red, Graphite Green.

9-3 Turbo X SportWagon KEY DIFFERENCES

NUMBER PRODUCED: 2000 (both body styles).
PRICE (UK – 2008): £33,595.
ENGINE: Transversely-mounted 60-degree V6 petrol, aluminium alloy cylinder head and block, four overhead camshafts (two per bank), four valves per cylinder with variable valve timing. Mitsubishi twin-scroll turbocharger with intercooler, running 0.8bar (11.6psi) boost. **Bore:** 89mm; **stroke:** 74.8mm; **capacity:** 2792cc. **Compression ratio:** 9.5:1; **maximum power:** 280bhp (DIN) at 5500rpm; **maximum torque:** 400Nm (295lb·ft) at 2150-4500rpm.
TRANSMISSION: Four-wheel drive, six-speed

manual or six-speed automatic transmission. Electronically-controlled limited-slip differential. **Final drive ratio:** 3.77:1.
BRAKES: Ventilated discs at front and rear. TCS and ESP standard.
WHEELS & TYRES: 7.5J x 19in, 235/40 ZR 19 tyres.
SUSPENSION: Uprated, with stiffened and lowered springs and recalibrated shock absorbers.
STEERING: Turning circle: 11.7m (38ft).
DIMENSIONS: Length: 4.67m (184in); **width:** 1.76m (69in); **height:** 1.50m (59in).
KERB WEIGHT: 1815kg (4001lb).
CAPACITIES: Fuel: 58 litres (12.8gal); **boot:** 419 litres (14.8ft^3), 1273 litres (45.0ft^3) with rear seats folded.
PERFORMANCE FIGURES: Top speed (limited): 155mph (250km/h); **0-62mph (100km/h):** 6.5sec; **overall fuel consumption:** 21.1mpg (13.4 litres/100km).
COLOURS: Jet Black metallic only.

Cadillac BLS

This chapter closes with one of the most curious cars ever built at Trollhättan. Saab was no stranger to badge engineering, whether with the Saab-Lancia 600 in the 1980s or the 9-2X, 9-4X and 9-7X models devised by GM's product planners in its final decade. The BLS, however, was a Saab reinvented as a Cadillac. Officially the 'B-segment Luxury Sedan', it was sometimes nicknamed the 'Bob Lutz Special', after GM's product czar. Never sold in North America, it was promoted as a compact executive car to bring the Cadillac brand into new markets, including continental Europe and the UK (where it was available with right-hand drive).

The BLS went on sale in March 2006, initially in saloon form only, with an estate (the BLS Wagon) following for 2007. Three trim levels were offered: SE, Luxury (with 17in alloy wheels, climate control and added convenience features) and Sport Luxury (with 18in alloys and sport-tuned suspension).

Mechanically, the Cadillac was closely based on the second-generation 9-3 in almost every way, although the suspension was revised and there were special subframes and extra sound deadening for enhanced comfort and refinement. There was a choice at launch of the 1.9-litre 16-valve turbodiesel and three turbocharged petrol engines: the 2.0-litre Ecotec 'four', developing either 175bhp or 210bhp (DIN), and the 250bhp (DIN) 2.8 V6. For the 2008 model year, a 200bhp (DIN) 2.0-litre Flexpower engine (able to run on E85) and the 180bhp diesel were added to the range. Manual and automatic transmissions with either five or six speeds were available, as on the equivalent 9-3 models.

The bodywork, however, was unique to the BLS, with a sharp-edged look and lights designed to resemble other Cadillac models. The interior was also given a makeover, with a new centre console and revised instrument cluster, along with real walnut veneer on the Luxury and Sport Luxury versions.

Not helped by Cadillac's small dealer network in Europe, the BLS never really found its place in the market and production came to an end after only three years, in August 2009.

The chiselled looks of the BLS were quite different from the Saab 9-3.

The square-cut rear end of the BLS Wagon, here a 2.8 V6.

BLS 1.9 TiD Sedan

NUMBER PRODUCED: 5911 (Sedan – all models); 1445 (Wagon – all models).
PRICE (UK – 2006): £25,073 (Luxury).
ENGINE: Four-cylinder in-line turbodiesel, mounted transversely, cast iron block and aluminium cylinder head, water-cooled with electric fan, dual overhead camshafts, four valves per cylinder. Bosch Motronic engine management system and common-rail direct fuel-injection, Garrett turbocharger with intercooler. **Bore:** 82.0mm; **stroke:** 90.4mm; **capacity:** 1910cc. **Compression ratio:** 17.5:1, **maximum power:** 148bhp (DIN) at 4000rpm; **maximum torque:** 320Nm (236lb·ft) at 2000rpm.
TRANSMISSION: Front-wheel drive, six-speed all-synchromesh manual gearbox with floor change. **Final drive ratio:** 3.55:1. Six-speed automatic transmission optional.
BRAKES: Ventilated discs at front and rear. Diagonal dual-circuit hydraulic system. ABS, EBD and Brake Assist. Stabilitrak ESP system and TCS standard in UK.
WHEELS & TYRES: 7J x 17in, 225/45 R 17 tyres.
SUSPENSION: Front: MacPherson struts with lower wishbones and coil springs; **rear:** fully independent multi-link, with coil springs. Anti-roll bars at front and rear.
STEERING: Rack and pinion with power assistance; **turning circle:** 10.9m (36ft).
DIMENSIONS: Length: 4.68m (184in); **width:** 1.75m (69in); **height:** 1.47m (58in); **wheelbase:** 2.68m (105in); **track:** front 1.52m (60in), rear 1.51m (59in).
KERB WEIGHT: 1460kg (3219lb).
CAPACITIES: Fuel: 58 litres (12.8gal); **boot:** 425 litres (15.0ft^3).
PERFORMANCE FIGURES: Top speed: 127mph (204km/h); **0-60mph (96km/h):** 9.5sec; **overall fuel consumption:** 35mpg (8 litres/100km).

The BLS had a different centre console with conventional cup-holders; the ignition key moved up to the steering column.

SAAB 9000

As the 1970s drew to a close, Saab was about to launch the 900, building on the success achieved by its pioneering 99 Turbo. But the company had ambitions to go further and enter the executive car market with a larger model. After possible merger talks with Volvo had broken down, in October 1978 Saab entered into an agreement with the Italian car makers Fiat, Alfa Romeo and Lancia to develop a series of saloons that would sit at the top of each manufacturer's range. The intention of the project – known as Tipo Quattro or Type Four – was to use a common front-wheel drive platform and a shared central bodyshell in order to reduce each company's development costs.

Between 1984 and 1987, each manufacturer introduced its own Type Four model: first, the Lancia Thema (the only one later also produced as an estate, known as the SW) and the Saab 9000, then the Fiat Croma and, finally, the Alfa Romeo 164. Each of the Italian cars would have its own personality and positioning in the market: the Fiat would be a more basic family hatchback and the Alfa Romeo the sportiest (helped by its celebrated V6 'Busso' engines), while the Lancia would offer a mix of refined performance and luxury. Saab, for its part, was keen to showcase its turbocharged, 16-valve engine and win new customers for the brand.

In practice, however, the differences between the four cars were far more extensive and they had only a handful of major components in common. Alfa Romeo shared only the chassis with the other models. The three Italian cars all featured independent MacPherson struts at both front and rear, but the Saab used a rigid rear axle. Although the central bodyshell of the Fiat, Lancia and Saab looked similar, Saab had to re-engineer the front of the car and strengthen the side-impact protection in the doors to meet American crash test requirements. Fortunately, despite these challenges in the development process, the outcome was a success and Saab went on to build more than half a million 9000s over a career lasting almost 14 years.

The 9000 was introduced to the press in Sweden in May 1984; it went on sale as

An early 9000 Turbo 16 in the Swedish winter.

Above: The Lancia Thema was announced in 1984; this photo shows a second-series saloon.
Right: A classic marketing shot of the 9000 Turbo 16.

Like the Saab 9000, the Fiat Croma was a roomy five-door hatchback.

The Alfa Romeo 164 was styled by Pininfarina.

Saab 9000 bodyshells in the paint shop in 1985.

This cutaway drawing by Rony Lutz shows the side-impact protection Saab had to add to the basic Type Four design.

a 1985 model in Europe and for the 1986 model year in the US. To begin with, it was available only as the five-door Turbo 16 hatchback, with a five-speed manual the sole transmission available. Saab promoted its prodigious in-gear acceleration above all as an aid to safety, and the 9000 also boasted seatbelt pretensioners, another Saab innovation.

Although it was 12cm (4.7in) shorter overall than the 900, the 9000 had shorter front and rear overhangs and a longer wheelbase, giving it better balanced looks and greater interior space. The design was the work of the renowned Italian designer Giorgetto Giugiaro, with input from Saab's Björn Envall, and the body achieved a creditable Cd figure of 0.33.

For 1986, Saab added the 9000i 16 to its range worldwide, with a naturally aspirated version of its 16-valve engine developing 130bhp (DIN). On the Turbo 16, wider-section (205/55) tyres were fitted.

In October that year, Saab proved the performance credentials of the 9000 Turbo 16 when it set two world records and 21 international speed records at the Talladega Speedway in Alabama. The fastest car covered 100,000km (62,137mi) at an average speed of 213.299km/h (132.538mph). Saab celebrated this achievement in Sweden with the Talladega limited edition in 1988: the engine was uprated from 175 to 192bhp (without a catalytic converter) and the car had firmer sports suspension. It was available only in black, with matching leather upholstery. Saab offered numerous other

The 9000 Turbo 16's B202L engine developed 175bhp (DIN).

The so-called 'marriage point' on the 9000 assembly line, when the body and drivetrain came together.

special editions with a similar specification in different markets, including the 9000 Turbo 16 SP in France and later the Carlsson in the UK.

For the 1987 model year, a four-speed ZF automatic transmission was available as an option. ABS (developed with Teves in Germany) became standard on the Turbo 16. The following year, all models were fitted with a basic trip computer.

The most important development in 1988, however, was the introduction of the 9000 CD four-door saloon, with a traditional boot and a more sloping front end. The CD was positioned above the five-door model, and in the UK it was initially sold only with the turbocharged engine, the naturally aspirated version following a year later. For 1990, a luxury CDE model was offered in the UK and

A Swedish-market Talladega special edition from 1988.

The original 9000 Turbo 16 seen in profile.

The 9000 CD was a classically styled three-box saloon.

some other markets, with standard equipment including automatic transmission, leather upholstery and automatic climate control. Also in the UK, the specialist coachbuilder Coleman Milne built a stretched limousine based on the 9000 CD.

There had been small power increases to both engines in 1989 to offset the power lost by the fitment of catalytic converters, but for the 1990 model year, Saab introduced a new 2.3-litre naturally aspirated engine with twin balancer shafts, designated B234, developing 150bhp (DIN). For the following model year, Saab fitted a turbocharger to the 2.3-litre engine, with 200bhp (DIN) and torque of 330Nm (243lb·ft) the impressive outcome.

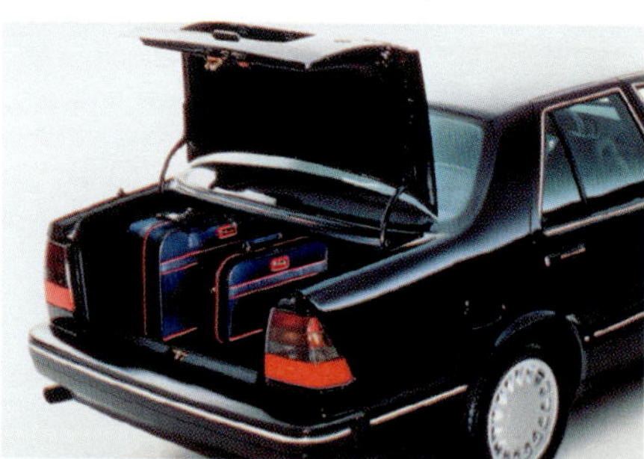

The CD had a generous boot capacity of 556 litres (19.6ft³).

By autumn 1991, however, the 9000 had been on sale for seven years, and it was time for it to receive a more thorough makeover. The five-door hatchback was renamed the 9000 CS/CSE (for Combi Sedan) and given a new, more rounded front end and, arguably less successfully, a higher tail; the engines on offer ranged from the 130bhp naturally aspirated 2.0-litre up to the 200bhp 2.3-litre turbo. In Sweden, the original five-door hatchback briefly continued as a base model known as the CC (for Combi Coupé) until the 1993 model year.

For 1992, a special edition of the four-door saloon known as the Turbo CD Griffin was offered in the US. Just 400 examples of this were produced, but the Griffin name was subsequently applied to the top-of-the-range four-door, first in North America and then in Europe as well.

The overall proportions of the CD were very similar to those of the five-door.

The facelifted 9000 CS had a steeply slanted front end.

The B234 engines had Saab's Direct Ignition system.

In October 1992, Saab unveiled what many consider to be the ultimate 9000 model, the 9000 CS Aero 2.3 Turbo. This had a distinctive bodykit with front and rear spoilers and 16in three-spoke alloy wheels; inside, the Aero had special Recaro-type seats with extra lateral support and exclusive leather upholstery. The suspension was lowered and uprated, with stiffer anti-roll bars and ZR-rated tyres. For cars with manual transmission, the 2.3-litre engine was boosted by a Mitsubishi TD04 turbocharger and developed

The Ecosport prototype from 1992 (inset) was very close to the production CS Aero 2.3 Turbo.

The capacious luggage compartment of a 1995 CSE.

225bhp (DIN) and a massive 342Nm (252lb·ft) of torque; cars with automatic transmission used a Garrett T25 turbocharger and developed slightly less power and torque.

For the 1993 model year, there were changes lower down the range as well. The base engine was a new 2.0-litre light-pressure turbo (LPT) unit, developing 150bhp (DIN), which offered greater mid-range torque. Known as 'Ecopower' in some markets, the new engine was available on both the CS and CD models. Saab progressively improved the level of equipment offered on the 9000, with a driver's airbag, electric windows and mirrors becoming standard equipment across the range. For 1994, the Saab Information Display, as seen on the 900 NG, was introduced on the 9000 as well.

North America remained a key market for Saab throughout the 1990s, but the 9000 had only been powered by four-cylinder engines since it was launched. For 1995, Saab therefore installed the 3.0-litre version of GM's 'Ellesmere V6' under the bonnet of the 9000. Built at GM's plant at Ellesmere Port in northern England, the B308 unit was also fitted to the Vauxhall/Opel Omega. For the 9000, however, it was mounted transversely rather than longitudinally. The V6 developed 210bhp (DIN) and traction control was standard. It sold mainly with a four-speed automatic gearbox, and although it was slower than the 2.3-litre turbocharged models, it was a refined cruiser, well suited to its primary market in the US. The 3.0 V6 proved a relatively slow seller, however, and was dropped after only two years in some markets.

Also for 1995, the CD and CDE four-door saloons received the same steeply raked front end that the five-door CS and CSE had been given when they were facelifted

The seats in the CS Aero 2.3 Turbo were probably the best ever fitted to a Saab.

The cockpit of a 1995 Aero; the overall design of the dashboard changed little during the 9000's career.

in autumn 1991. The model range now on offer in the UK comprised the CS, CSE and Aero five-door models, and the CD, CDE and Griffin booted saloons. The CSE and CDE variants had additional standard equipment such as automatic climate control and a walnut veneer fascia. The 170bhp (DIN) 2.3 LPT Ecopower engine, introduced for 1996, probably represented a happy medium for these mainstream models.

In 1997, Saab celebrated 50 years since the presentation of what it humorously described as its "first earth-bound model" with several limited-edition models. These included the 'Jubileum' in Sweden and the Anniversary Edition in the UK. The UK model, which was available with three different engines, had special eight-spoke alloy wheels, colour-keyed bumpers and bodykit, a walnut dashboard and two-tone leather seats embossed with Saab's historic propellor logo.

By now, however, the new 9-5 was waiting in the wings, and for its final model year in 1998, Saab discontinued many models in the 9000 range. In the US, only two versions of the CSE remained on sale: the last Aero Turbos and a special CSE Turbo, which had the 225bhp Aero engine, but not its stiffer suspension.

A lovely Ruby Red 3.0 V6 CSE from 1995.

The B308 V6 engine installed in the 9000.

This 1993 9000 CDE and the 1995 9000 Griffin show the changes made to the front of the four-door model.

Below: Saab GB produced this special brochure for its 9000 Anniversary Edition in 1997.

9000 Turbo 16

NUMBER PRODUCED: 503,087 (all models).
PRICE (UK – 1985): £15,995.
ENGINE: Four-cylinder in-line petrol, mounted transversely, cast iron block and aluminium cylinder head, five main bearings, water-cooled with electric fan, dual chain-driven overhead camshafts and four valves per cylinder. Bosch LH-Jetronic fuel-injection with Automatic Performance Control and Garrett T3 turbocharger with intercooler, running 0.85bar (12.3psi) boost. **Bore:** 90mm; **stroke:** 78mm; **capacity:** 1985cc. **Compression ratio:** 9.0:1; **maximum power:** 175bhp (DIN) at 5300rpm; **maximum torque:** 273Nm (201lb·ft) at 3000rpm.
TRANSMISSION: Front-wheel drive, five-speed all-synchromesh manual gearbox with floor change. **Final drive ratio:** 4.21:1. Four-speed ZF automatic transmission optional from 1987.
BRAKES: Ventilated discs at front and rear.

Diagonal dual-circuit hydraulic system. ABS standard from 1987.
WHEELS & TYRES: 6J x 15in, 205/55 VR 15 radial-ply tyres.
SUSPENSION: Front: MacPherson struts with lower wishbones and coil springs; **rear:** rigid axle with multi-link arms, coil springs and Panhard rod. Anti-roll bars at front and rear.
STEERING: Rack and pinion with power assistance; **turning circle:** 10.9m (36ft).
ELECTRICAL SYSTEM: 12-volt; **battery capacity:** 62Ah.
DIMENSIONS: Length: 4.62m (182in); **width:** 1.76m (69in); **height:** 1.42m (56in); **wheelbase:** 2.67m (105in); **track:** front 1.52m (60in), rear 1.49m (59in).
KERB WEIGHT: 1325kg (2921lb).
CAPACITIES: Fuel: 68 litres (15.0gal); **boot:** 450 litres (15.9ft^3), 1600 litres (56.5ft^3) with rear seats folded.
PERFORMANCE FIGURES: Top speed: 138mph (222km/h); **0-60mph (96km/h):** 8.3sec; overall fuel consumption: 22.7mpg (12.4 litres/100km).
COLOURS (1987): (solid) Cirrus White, Embassy Blue, Cherry, Rodonite Red, Black; (metallic) Silver, Malachite, Bronze, Magenta Brown, Odoardo (in US: Edwardian Gray), Rose Quartz, Platinum.

9000 CS Aero 2.3 Turbo
KEY DIFFERENCES

PRICE (UK – 1995): £29,995.
ENGINE: Twin contra-rotating balancer shafts, Saab Trionic engine management system and Mitsubishi TD04 turbocharger with intercooler, running 1.08bar (15.7psi) boost (with manual transmission)/Garrett T25 turbocharger with intercooler, running 0.81bar (11.7psi) boost (with automatic transmission). **Bore:** 90mm, **stroke:** 90mm, **capacity:** 2290cc. **Compression ratio:** 9.25:1; **maximum power:** 225bhp (DIN) at 5500rpm (manual)/200bhp (DIN) at 5500rpm (auto); **maximum torque:** 342Nm (252lb·ft) at 1800rpm (manual)/294Nm (217lb·ft) at 1800rpm (auto).
TRANSMISSION: Final drive ratio: 3.61:1.
BRAKES: Traction Control System (TCS) standard on cars with manual transmission.
WHEELS & TYRES: 6.5J x 16in, 205/55 ZR 16 tyres.
DIMENSIONS: Length: 4.76m (187in); **width:**1.78m (70in); **height:** 1.42m (56in); **wheelbase:** 2.67m (105in); **track:** front 1.52m (60in), rear 1.49m (59in).
KERB WEIGHT: 1440kg (3175lb).
CAPACITIES: Fuel: 66 litres (14.5gal); **boot:** 487 litres (49.3ft^3), 1397 litres (56.5ft^3) with rear seats folded.
PERFORMANCE FIGURES: Top speed: 149mph (240km/h); **0-60mph (96km/h):** 6.7sec; **overall fuel consumption:** 29.2mpg (9.7 litres/100km). All figures with manual transmission.

9000 CD 3.0 V6 Griffin
KEY DIFFERENCES

PRICE (UK – 1995): £29,995.
ENGINE: Naturally aspirated, transversely mounted 54-degree V6 petrol, four overhead camshafts (two per bank). Motronic M2.8.1 engine management system with multi-point fuel-injection. **Bore:** 86mm; **stroke:** 85mm; **capacity:** 2962cc. **Compression ratio:** 10.8:1; **maximum power:** 210bhp (DIN) at 6200rpm; **maximum torque:** 270Nm (199lb·ft) at 3300rpm.
TRANSMISSION: Four-speed automatic transmission with floor change standard on Griffin, five-speed manual also available on 3.0 V6 CSE. **Final drive ratio:** 3.57:1 (auto).
BRAKES: Traction Control System (TCS) standard.
WHEELS & TYRES: 6J x 15in cross-spoke alloys, 195/65 R 15 tyres.
DIMENSIONS: Length: 4.79m (189in); other dimensions as 9000 CS Aero 2.3 Turbo.
KERB WEIGHT: 1475kg (3252lb).
CAPACITIES: Fuel: 66 litres (14.5gal); **boot:** 556 litres (19.6ft^3).
PERFORMANCE FIGURES: Top speed: 140mph (225km/h); **0-60mph (96km/h):** 9.0sec; **overall fuel consumption:** 24.8mpg (11.4 litres/100km). All figures with automatic transmission.
COLOURS (1995): (solid) Black, Cirrus White, Imola Red, Embassy Blue; (metallic) Citrin Beige, Silver, Ruby Red, Scarabe Green, Eucalyptus Green, Aubergine, Le Mans Blue.

Two late-model 9000s from 1997: a CSE (red) and Aero (silver).

SAAB 9-5 AND 9-5 NG

Saab 9-5

Saab's first foray into the larger executive car market had been a success, and the company was keen to build on the positive results achieved by the 9000. Saab began by talking to Fiat with a view to updating the Alfa Romeo 164 platform, one of the Type Four family of cars. In the end, this proposal came to naught and Saab's new large car was developed – in less than four years – on a lengthened version of GM's Vectra platform. Known internally as Project 640, it was badged as the 9^5 and always promoted as the 9-5 (pronounced 'nine-five'), in line with the 9-3.

Despite the short lead time and recourse to GM underpinnings, the 9-5 still came across as distinct from GM's other Vauxhall/Opel models, with an emphasis on comfort, safety, performance and aerodynamic efficiency, as was characteristic of the Swedish firm. For the first time on a Saab, the 9-5 had a sophisticated, fully independent multi-link rear suspension.

The 9-5 was designed in-house by Einar Hareide and Tony Catignani; the curved windscreen and swept rear window had echoes of older Saab models right back to the 99 and it achieved a drag coefficient as low as 0.29. The wraparound dashboard and joystick controls for the air vents were also familiar design touches inside the new model. Even the ignition key found its way back between the front seats!

The new model was formally introduced at

The 9-5 undergoing testing in simulated winter conditions during its development.

One of the first 9-5s in final assembly at Trollhättan in 1997.

The original 9-5 Saloon.

The 9-5 Saloon, seen in profile in this illustration by Rony Lutz.

Håkan Danielsson was in charge of aerodynamic testing of the 9 5.

The dashboard of the 9-5; earlier models had this four-spoke steering wheel.

Trollhättan in June 1997, before its European launch at the Frankfurt Motor Show in September that year. The 9-5 and 9-3 then made their joint US debut at the Detroit Auto Show in January 1998. It was initially available as a three-box four-door Saloon (or Sedan in the US) with a 60:40 split-folding rear seat, a direct successor to the 9000 CD/CDE. Unlike the 9000, however, the 9-5 was never produced as a hatchback.

Instead, a spacious estate model was unveiled in May 1998 and presented at the Paris Motor Show in September that year. This was known variously as the Estate in the UK, the SportWagon in the US, the SportEstate in Australia and the SportKombi in Germany. It proved popular with families and antique dealers alike. Viewers of the Swedish crime series *Wallander* will have seen the 9-5 Estate in service with the local police on the streets of Ystad; it was also used by police forces in England and Scotland, often in 'HOT' (High Output Turbo) Aero spec, as well as in several other European countries and the US.

The range of engines at launch centred around two four-cylinder petrol units with light-pressure turbos: a 2.0-litre developing 150bhp (DIN) and a 2.3-litre producing 170bhp (DIN). Both engines used the latest version of Saab's Trionic engine management system and had four valves per cylinder, dual overhead camshafts and twin balancer shafts. As usual, they could be supplied with a five-speed manual gearbox or four-speed automatic transmission.

Early in 1998, these were joined by the 3.0t V6 Ecopower, an evolution of GM's naturally-aspirated 3.0-litre V6 installed in the 9000. In the 9-5, however, the engine was turbocharged, with an innovative asymmetrical design whereby the exhaust gases from one bank of cylinders drove the light-pressure turbo, which then boosted both banks. The result was a torquey engine which played to Saab's traditional reputation for the effective use of turbocharging. It was available only with automatic transmission.

A Black 9-5 Estate from the first year of production.

A UK Police-spec 2.3 HOT Estate from 2007.

The 9-5 also upheld Saab's reputation when it came to safety. The body structure incorporated a central 'safety cage' for the occupants, front and rear crumple zones, and specially reinforced door pillars designed to direct crash forces away from the passengers. For both the 9-3 and 9-5, Saab introduced its 'Active Head Restraints' (SAHR), designed to reduce whiplash injures. Side and head airbags were part of the new model's standard equipment from the start, along with the company's 'Night Panel' feature, also seen on the 9-3. The 9-5's sills and A-pillars were further strengthened in 2002, so that even a decade after its introduction, the 9-5 remained one of the safest cars on the road.

For 1999, Saab reintroduced the Griffin name for its range-topping V6 Saloon. Intended to compete with the new Volvo S80 as well as the German premium makes, this luxury model had automatic climate control, a walnut veneer dashboard and leather upholstery. For the first time on a production model, the 9-5's electrically adjustable front seats could be ventilated as well as heated, and these came as standard on the Griffin.

In September 1999, it was the turn of the high-performance Aero version to make its reappearance, with three-spoke 17in alloy wheels, sports suspension and a distinctive bodykit. It was powered by a 2.3-litre High Output Turbo engine which developed 230bhp (DIN) and – when paired with the five-speed manual transmission – maximum torque of 350Nm (258lb·ft) from 1900-4000rpm. An 'overboost' function, available for 20 seconds (when overtaking, for example), saw peak

Two 9-5s undergoing an offset frontal crash test.

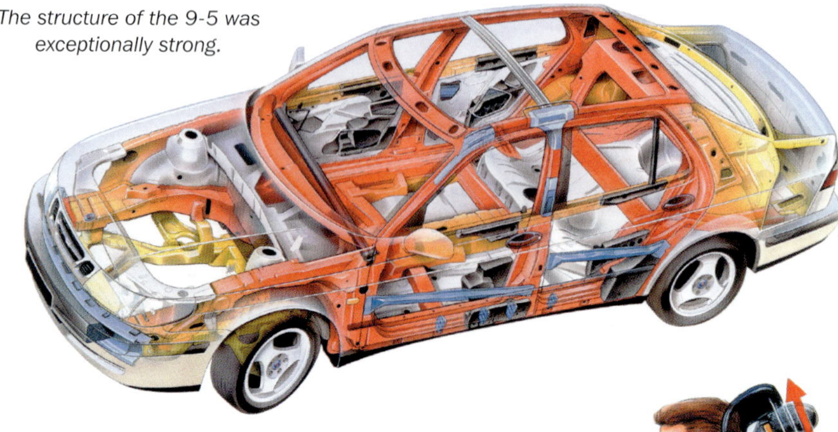
The structure of the 9-5 was exceptionally strong.

torque rise momentarily to 370Nm (273lb·ft). Saab's Traction Control System (TCS) was a welcome standard fitment.

Also new for the 2000 model year, Saab Parking Assistance became available as an option. For the following model year (2001), the 2.3t Ecopower engine was uprated from 170 to 185bhp.

2002 marked the first major milestone in the life cycle of the 9-5, when it was given a facelift with an integrated single-piece grille and front bumper, new headlamps and revised taillamps. The earlier S and SE trim levels were replaced by Linear (described by Saab as "refined, unadorned and taut"), Arc ("modern and classic") and Vector ("exuding performance and dynamics"). The Aero continued as the top high-performance version, with power increasing to 250bhp (DIN). ESP (electronic stability control) became available as an option, while a much more modern, five-speed automatic transmission

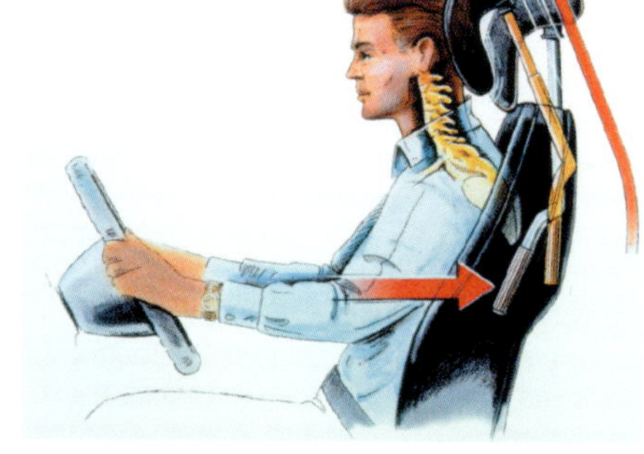
The 9-5 was equipped with Saab's first-generation Active Head Restraints.

The luxurious interior of the 9 5 with ventilated seats in perforated Sand leather.

A facelifted 9-5 Estate from 2002, showing the new front end.

replaced the original four-speed unit. Christened Saab Sentronic, from 2003 this could also be overridden using paddles on the steering wheel.

In the executive class, as well as lower down the range, diesel engines were critical in European markets such as France and Belgium, and for 2002 Saab introduced an entirely new 3.0 TiD turbodiesel producing 176bhp (DIN) and 350Nm (258lb·ft). It was an all-aluminium V6 developed jointly with Isuzu (which was part-owned by GM). Later in 2002, Saab added the 125bhp (DIN) four-cylinder 2.2 TiD already offered on the first-generation 9-3 as a more economical alternative.

For the 2003 model year, TCS was fitted as standard to nearly all models and a DVD-based touch-screen satellite navigation system was listed as an optional extra. The following year, there were some important changes to the engine line-up. The 3.0 V6 petrol engine was dropped. To bridge the gap between the 2.3t and 2.3 Aero models, a 2.3 Turbo developing 220bhp (DIN) was added to the range, but without the sports suspension and brushed aluminium interior trim specific to the Aero.

An Aero Saloon from 2004.

From the side, the changes to the facelifted model – here a 2003 Aero Estate –were less noticeable.

Two years later, for the 2006 model year, Saab introduced the second and final facelift of the 9-5, with revised front and rear styling. Always a difficult exercise to carry off, the results proved controversial. At the front, the chrome grille surround and headlamp trims mimicked the spectacles worn by the Australian performer Barry Humphries, earning the final cars the unfortunate nickname 'Dame Edna'. The interior was updated at the same time, with new instruments and simplified heating and air-conditioning controls (similar to those on the revised 9-3), as well as a more sophisticated Saab Infotainment System on higher-spec models. The Aero was fitted with a new design of leather sports seats.

From 2006 onwards, there were more changes to the range of engines available. The Aero gained another 10bhp, for a new maximum of 260bhp (DIN), while both the four-cylinder and V6 diesels were replaced by the 150bhp (DIN) 1.9 TiD engine supplied by Fiat that was also fitted to the smaller 9-3.

Of more significance perhaps was the arrival for the 2006 model year of the eco-friendly 2.0t BioPower, based on Saab's

"Hello, Possums!" The front of the 9-5 Aero Saloon following its final facelift in 2006.

The revised 9-5 seen from the rear: note the body-coloured door handles.

The facelifted Estate had the same frontal treatment as the Saloon..

The final 9-5 models had a much simpler centre console and a three-spoke steering wheel.

The 1.9 TiD turbodiesel was Euro 4-compliant.

light-pressure turbo engine. Both Saloon and Estate versions were offered. The BioPower engines were optimised to use bioethanol (E85), with an output of 180bhp (DIN), but could also run on regular petrol, albeit with a 14 per cent drop in power. The advanced Saab Trionic engine management system automatically compensated for any combination of bioethanol and petrol, and Saab claimed that these engines cut CO_2 emissions by up to 70 per cent when running on bioethanol compared to petrol. For 2007, a 2.3-litre BioPower model was added; when using bioethanol, this produced 210bhp (DIN).

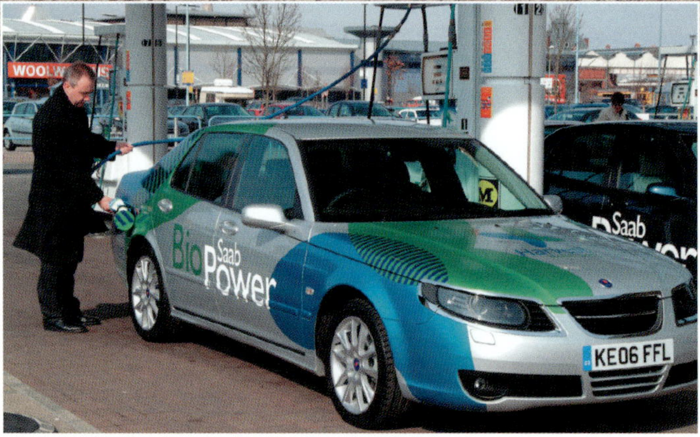

Marketing logos aside, only a small BioPower badge at the rear identified the new model.

Left: Filling up a BioPower Saloon with bioethanol at a supermarket fuel station in the UK.

The Anniversary Edition Estate looked especially stylish in Ice Blue metallic.

For the final years of its career, as the 9-5 aged and Saab struggled to keep going as a business, there were minor changes to the interior trim and a number of limited editions of both the Saloon and Estate, including the Anniversary Edition in 2007 and, in the UK, the Turbo and Aero Turbo Editions in 2008. Both the Anniversary and Turbo Editions featured leather sports seats and distinctive alloy wheels; the Anniversary model was also offered in a special Ice Blue colour. Alongside Saab's own special editions, several companies, including Abbott Racing in the UK, Hirsch in Switzerland and Maptun in Sweden, offered tuning parts and cosmetic upgrades for the 9-5.

A UK-market Turbo Edition Estate from 2008.

In 2008, the range of engines was rationalised, leaving in the UK the 150bhp 2.0t and 1.9 TiD, the 180bhp 2.0t BioPower, 210bhp 2.3t BioPower and 260bhp 2.3T Aero.

For its ultimate model year in 2009, the 9-5 – now sometimes referred to as the 9-5 OG (for 'original generation') – was designated Griffin in several markets. The last Saloon was built on July 2, 2009, followed by the final Estate on February 1, 2010. The turbulent history of both Saab and GM during the 2000s resulted in the 9-5 remaining on sale for much longer than was planned, but it was far from a failure, with nearly half a million cars produced.

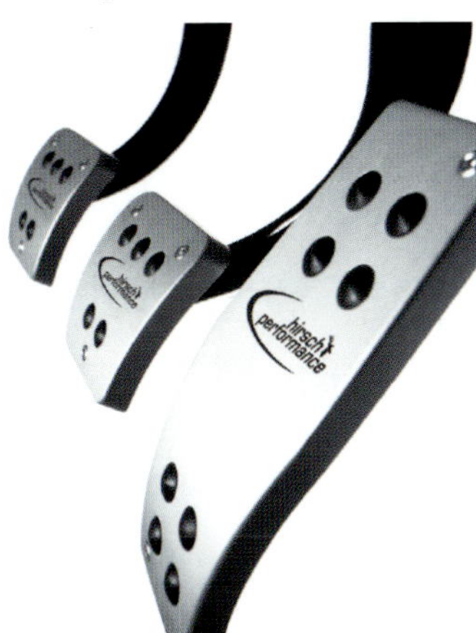

Parts from the Hirsch Performance Programme, like these alloy pedals, were officially approved by Saab.

9-5 3.0t V6 Ecopower Saloon (2000)

NUMBER PRODUCED: Saloon: 252,236; **Estate:** 231,357 (all models).
PRICE (UK): £33,995 (Griffin).
ENGINE: Transversely-mounted 54-degree V6 petrol, cast iron block and aluminium cylinder head, four overhead camshafts (two per bank) and four valves per cylinder. Saab Trionic 7 engine management system with fuel-injection and Garrett GT17 turbocharger with intercooler, running 0.25bar (3.6psi) boost. Three-way catalytic converter and Lambda sensor. **Bore:** 86mm; **stroke:** 85mm; **capacity:** 2962cc. **Compression ratio:** 9.5:1; **maximum power:** 200bhp (DIN) at 5000rpm; **maximum torque:** 310Nm (229lb·ft) at 2100rpm.
TRANSMISSION: Four-speed ZF automatic transmission with floor change and three programs. **Final drive ratio:** 2.55:1.
BRAKES: Power-assisted discs all round (ventilated at front). Diagonal split circuit. ABS, EBD (Electronic Brake-force Distribution) and Traction Control System (TCS) standard.

WHEELS & TYRES: 6J x 16in, 215/55 VR 16 tyres.
SUSPENSION: Front: MacPherson spring struts with twin-tube gas-filled shock absorbers; **rear:** independent multi-link axle with coil springs and gas-filled shock absorbers. Anti-roll bars at front and rear.
STEERING: Rack and pinion with power assistance; **turning circle:** 10.8m (35ft).
ELECTRICAL SYSTEM: 12-volt; **battery capacity:** 70Ah.
DIMENSIONS: Length: 4.81m (189in); **width:** 1.79m (71in); **height:** 1.45m (57in); **wheelbase:** 2.70m (106in); **track (front & rear):** 1.52m (60in).
KERB WEIGHT: 1618kg (3567lb).
CAPACITIES: Fuel: 70 litres (15.4gal); **boot:** 500 litres (17.7ft^3).
PERFORMANCE FIGURES: Top speed: 146mph (235km/h); **0-60mph (96km/h):** 8.8sec; **overall fuel consumption:** 21-23mpg (12-13 litres/100km).
COLOURS: Solid: Black, Imola Red, Cirrus White, Embassy Blue; metallic: Sun Green, Cayenne Red, Midnight Blue, Cosmic Blue, Silver, Scarabe Green, Frost Grey, Morello Red.

9-5 3.0 V6 TiD Estate (2002)
KEY DIFFERENCES

PRICE (UK): £27,595 (Vector).
ENGINE: Transversely-mounted 66-degree V6 turbodiesel, light-alloy block and cylinder head, four overhead camshafts (two per bank) and four valves per cylinder. Common-rail direct fuel-injection and Garrett variable-geometry turbocharger with intercooler and exhaust gas recirculation (EGR). **Bore:** 87.5mm; **stroke:** 82mm; **capacity:** 2958cc. **Compression ratio:** 18.0:1; **maximum power:** 176bhp (DIN) at 4000rpm; **maximum torque:** 350Nm (258lb·ft) at 1800-3000rpm.
TRANSMISSION: Front-wheel drive, five-speed all-synchromesh manual gearbox with floor change. **Final drive ratio:** 3.81:1. Five-speed automatic transmission optional.
BRAKES: Traction Control System (TCS) standard from 2003 model year.
WHEELS & TYRES: 7J x 17in, 225/45 ZR 17 tyres (Vector).
ELECTRICAL SYSTEM: 12-volt; **battery capacity:** 85Ah.
DIMENSIONS: Length: 4.83m (190in); **width:** 1.79m (71in); **height:** 1.50m (59in); **wheelbase:** 2.70m (106in); **track (front & rear):** 1.52m (60in).
KERB WEIGHT: 1760kg (3880lb).
CAPACITIES: Fuel: 75 litres (16.5gal); **boot:** 416 litres (14.7ft^3), 1490 litres (52.6ft^3) with rear seats folded.
PERFORMANCE FIGURES: Top speed: 128mph (206km/h); **0-60mph (96km/h):** 8.2sec; **overall fuel consumption:** 35.3mpg (8 litres/100km).
COLOURS: Solid: Black, Laser Red, Polar White; metallic: Silver, Midnight Blue, Steel Grey, Cosmic Blue, Sun Green, Hazelnut.

9-5 2.3 HOT Aero Saloon (2006)
KEY DIFFERENCES

PRICE (UK): £28,336.
ENGINE: Four-cylinder in-line petrol, mounted transversely, cast iron block and aluminium cylinder head, dual overhead camshafts, four valves per cylinder and twin balancer shafts. Saab Trionic 7 engine management system with Bosch fuel-injection and Mitsubishi TD04 turbocharger with intercooler. **Bore:** 90mm; **stroke:** 90mm; **capacity:** 2290cc. **Compression ratio:** 9.25:1; **maximum power:** 260bhp (DIN) at 5300rpm; **maximum torque:** 350Nm (258lb·ft) at 1900rpm (370Nm/273lb·ft with overboost function (on manual transmission models).
TRANSMISSION: Front-wheel drive, five-speed all-synchromesh manual gearbox with floor change. **Final drive ratio:** 4.05:1. Five-speed Saab Sentronic automatic transmission optional.
BRAKES: Ventilated disc brakes at front and rear. Diagonal split circuit. ABS, EBD, TCS and ESP all standard.
WHEELS & TYRES: 7.5J x 17in, 235/45 ZR 17 tyres.
SUSPENSION: Uprated sports suspension.
DIMENSIONS: Length: 4.84m (190in).
KERB WEIGHT: 1610kg (3549lb).
PERFORMANCE FIGURES: Top speed: 155mph (250km/h); 0-62mph (100km/h): 6.9sec; **overall fuel consumption:** 28.5mpg (9.9 litres/100km).
COLOURS: Solid: Black, Laser Red, Polar White; metallic: Silver, Steel Grey, Nocturne Blue, Parchment Silver, Chilli Red, Smoke Beige, Jet Black, Fusion Blue, Arbor Green.

Saab 9-5 NG

It was surely a miracle that the second-generation 9-5 ever saw the light of day. The original 9-5 had enjoyed a long career and the first project to replace it had been cancelled in 2005, after GM and Fiat terminated their planned partnership. Despite all the turmoil surrounding Saab during the second half of the 2000s, the 9-5 NG nonetheless emerged at the Frankfurt Motor Show in September 2009. It was the final model developed under GM's ownership of Saab and was based on the Epsilon II platform, also used in the same lengthened version for the Buick LaCrosse in the US.

GM originally intended to build the new Saab at its Opel plant at Rüsselsheim in Germany, and 122 pre-production cars were assembled there before it was officially presented. At the end of 2009, however, GM announced that Saab would be wound up, only for it to be seized from the jaws of defeat by the Dutch supercar manufacturer Spyker. After a brief hiatus, pilot production of the 9-5 Saloon began at Trollhättan in March 2010 and sales commenced three months later. Saab put a brave face on things and talked proudly of the start of a new, independent era.

In many ways, the new car was a triumph. Styled by a team led by the British designer Simon Padian, the 9-5 had a low drag coefficient (0.28) and clean, elegant lines that have aged well. Its overall length of just over 5m (197in) was criticised by some European reviewers, but it ensured that the car was exceptionally roomy inside.

The interior was very similar to that of the 9-4X, and although components such as the column stalks were shared with the Opel/Vauxhall Insignia, over 70 per cent of all the parts were unique to Saab, no doubt to GM's dismay. Like every Saab, it had superb seats and design flourishes such as green instrument lighting (complete with a 'Night Panel' function), an altimeter-style speedometer display and Saab's traditional joystick controls for the air vents. The new 9-5 was also technologically far ahead of its predecessor, with an optional, aviation-inspired head-up display for the driver, dual-zone air-conditioning and a sophisticated Harman Kardon audio system, as well as keyless entry and adaptive bi-xenon headlights.

In North America, the 9-5 Sedan (as

The very first 9-5 down the line at Trollhättan on 22 March 2010 was destined to join a test fleet.

Front and rear views of a 9-5 Turbo4 XWD Aero Saloon.

it was known there) was available with two turbocharged petrol engines, a 2.0-litre 'four' producing 220bhp and a 2.8-litre V6 developing 300bhp (DIN). In Europe, the range of engines was wider, with an entry-level 1.6T petrol-engined model producing 180bhp and a pair of 2.0-litre turbodiesels: the 160bhp TiD and the 190bhp (DIN) TTiD. A BioPower version of the 2.0-litre turbo, running on bioethanol (E85), was also offered.

The chassis was the most advanced Saab had ever offered, with sophisticated 'HiPer' strut suspension geometry on the 2.0TTiD FWD and 2.8T XWD models, using a separate, steerable hub like that fitted to the Renault Sport Mégane. Adaptive dampers known as 'DriveSense' were also available. Drawing on Saab's experience with the 9-3 Turbo X, a Haldex four-wheel drive system (again

The interior of a 9-5 Saloon with Jet Black perforated leather seats.

A close-up view of the centre console of the 9-5.

The head-up display and altimeter-style speedo were new, but the turbo boost gauge had long been a Saab feature.

badged 'XWD') with an electronic limited-slip differential could be specified on the 2.0T and 2.8T.

Equipment levels varied by market: in North America, Saab offered the Turbo4, Turbo4 Premium, Turbo6 XWD and the top-of-the-range Aero XWD. In continental Europe, Saab applied its then customary model hierarchy, with Linear, Vector and Aero trims, while the UK opted to sell just two well-equipped versions: Vector SE and Aero.

Minor trim and equipment changes were made to the Saloon for the 2011 model year, and in March 2011 Saab unveiled the new 9-5 Estate (also known as the SportCombi, and as the SportWagon in the US). If anything, it was even better-looking than the Saloon, but it was also supremely

A 9-5 Saloon at speed in the Swedish winter.

The 9-5 Estate seen from the side and rear.

practical, with a power-operated tailgate, an adjustable U-rail cargo management system and aluminium roof rails. With the rear seats folded down, the luggage capacity increased from 527 litres (18.6ft³) to a massive 1600 litres (56.5ft³). The 9-5 Estate was due to go on sale in September 2011, but sadly, it never made it into series production, as Saab faced increasing liquidity problems during its final year. Just 33 protypes and pre-production cars were built.

Undaunted, Saab announced further improvements to come for 2012, including Adaptive Cruise Control and Start/Stop functionality to reduce fuel consumption and exhaust emissions. The company's financial situation continued to worsen, however, and the last 9-5s were built on 8 June 2011. GM blocked any attempts to sell the business and its proprietary technology to Chinese car makers, and in December 2011 Saab was forced to file for bankruptcy.

9-5 2.0T Saloon (2010)

NUMBER PRODUCED: 11,478 (all models).
PRICES (UK): £28,195 (Vector SE)/£31,195 (Aero).
ENGINE: Four-cylinder in-line petrol, mounted transversely, aluminium alloy cylinder head and block, water-cooled with electric fan, twin balancer shafts, dual overhead camshafts, four valves per cylinder with variable valve timing, Bosch Motronic MED direct fuel-injection and twin-scroll turbocharger with intercooler. Three-way catalytic converter and Lambda sensor. **Bore:** 86mm; **stroke:** 86mm; **capacity:** 1998cc. **Compression ratio:** 9.5:1; **maximum power:** 220bhp (DIN) at 5300rpm; **maximum torque:** 350Nm (258lb·ft) at 2500rpm.
TRANSMISSION: Front-wheel drive, six-speed all-synchromesh manual gearbox with floor change. **Final drive ratio:** 3.76:1. Six-speed Saab Sentronic automatic transmission with manual shift mode optional. Four-wheel drive (XWD) available on Aero.

BRAKES: Ventilated discs at front and rear. ABS, EBD, Brake Assist, TCS and ESP standard.
WHEELS & TYRES: 7J x 17in, 225/55 R 17 tyres (Vector); 8J x 18in, 245/45 R 18 tyres (Aero).
SUSPENSION: Front: MacPherson struts, coil springs and gas-filled shock absorbers; **rear:** fully independent, linked H-arm with coil springs and gas-filled shock absorbers (DriveSense adaptive dampers optional). Anti-roll bars at front and rear.
STEERING: Rack and pinion with hydraulic power assistance (variable rate on cars equipped with DriveSense or XWD); **turning circle:** 12.0m (39ft).
DIMENSIONS: Length: 5.01m (197in); **width:** 1.87m (73in); **height:** 1.47m (58in); **wheelbase:** 2.84m (112in); **track (front & rear):** 1.58m (62in).
KERB WEIGHT: 1655kg (3649lb).
CAPACITIES: Fuel: 70l (15.4gal); **boot:** 513 litres (18.1ft^3).
PERFORMANCE FIGURES: Top speed: 146mph (235km/h); **0-62mph (100km/h):** 8.3sec; **combined fuel consumption:** 29.1mpg (9.7 litres/100km). All figures with automatic transmission.
COLOURS: Solid: Arctic White, Laser Red, Black; metallic: Jet Black, Glacier Silver, Granite Grey, Fjord Blue, Carbon Grey, Diamond Silver, Oak, Java.

Saab planned to sell a range of accessories to match the active lifestyle of 9-5 Estate owners.

THE OTHER GM-ERA SAABS

Throughout most of the 1990s, Saab struggled to build and sell more than 100,000 cars a year, too few by far to ensure its long-term profitability. When GM took full control of the company in 2000, it needed to enter a wider range of market segments and massively increase its sales. Sadly, however, it was unable or unwilling to commit the resources needed to develop a compelling range of new cars, and the 9-2X, 9-4X and 9-7X models it launched during the 2000s were largely unconvincing examples of badge engineering.

For Saab loyalists especially – whose patience had already been tested by the second-generation 9-3 – the new cars were a travesty, betraying the values that had drawn them to the marque. The 9-5 NG, presented in the previous chapter, held out some hope for the future, but it was too little, too late.

Saab 9-2X

All three new models had four-wheel drive (hence their names ending in 'X'). The first, and smallest, was the 9-2X, a sporty five-door hatchback unveiled at the 2004 Detroit Auto Show. Saab had lacked a successful entry-level model ever since the venerable 96 went out of production in 1980, so the stakes could scarcely have been higher. Rather than adapt the platform used for its successful Vauxhall/Opel Astra, however, GM chose to enter the 'Premium Sport Compact' segment with a barely disguised version of the Subaru Impreza WRX Wagon. GM had acquired a 20 per cent stake in Subaru's parent company, Fuji Heavy Industries, in 1999 and saw an opportunity to introduce a new model at greatly reduced cost.

Saab made some modifications to the Impreza's suspension and steering for the 9-2X, but most of the changes were cosmetic. The bonnet scoop was made smaller, and both the front and rear of the car were restyled to align them more closely with Saab's other models. The interior was almost identical to the Subaru, although Saab fitted its own front seats incorporating its Active Head Restraints.

The 9-2X was only sold in North America and two versions were offered at launch: the Linear, with a 2.5-litre naturally aspirated four-cylinder 'boxer' engine developing 165bhp (SAE), and the Aero, with a 2.0-litre turbocharged 'boxer' unit producing 227bhp (SAE). For 2006, the Linear was renamed the 2.5i, while the 2.0-litre engine in the Aero

A 9-4X and 9-5 NG saloon photographed together in September 2010.

The Subaru Impreza WRX was sold in both four-and five-door form.

was replaced by a 2.5-litre turbo, with a small increase in power and torque.

Both versions could be ordered with a five-speed manual or four-speed automatic transmission. A range of option packs (Premium, Sport and Cold Weather) let customers add features such as leather upholstery, an electric sunroof and heated seats.

When the 9-2X launched, *Car and Driver* magazine gamely remarked: "It's like a swanky WRX that's better in every way." But the market was unconvinced by the car tagged the 'Saabaru' and it was discontinued after the 2006 model year.

9-2X Aero

NUMBER PRODUCED: 10,324 (all models).
PRICE AT LAUNCH (US): $26,950.
ENGINE: Four-cylinder petrol, mounted longitudinally with horizontally opposed cylinders, aluminium alloy cylinder head and block, water-cooled, dual overhead camshafts, four valves per cylinder, multi-point fuel-injection and turbocharger with intercooler. **Bore:** 92.0mm; **stroke:** 75.0mm; **capacity:** 1994cc. **Compression ratio:** 8.0:1; **maximum power:** 227bhp (SAE) at 6000rpm; **maximum torque:** 294Nm (217lb·ft) at 4000rpm.
TRANSMISSION: Four-wheel drive, five-speed all-synchromesh manual gearbox with floor change. **Final drive ratio:** 3.9:1. Four-speed automatic transmission optional.
BRAKES: Front: ventilated discs; **rear:** solid discs. ABS.
WHEELS & TYRES: 7J x 17in, 215/45 ZR 17 Bridgestone Potenza tyres.
SUSPENSION: Front: MacPherson struts and

Front and rear views of a 9-2X Aero from 2004.

This 9-2X Aero has fabric trim and the optional automatic transmission.

coil springs; **rear:** independent with trailing arms and coil springs. Anti-roll bars at front and rear.

STEERING: Rack and pinion with electro-hydraulic power assistance; **turning circle:** 10.8m (35ft).

ELECTRICAL SYSTEM: 12-volt; **battery capacity:** 52Ah.

DIMENSIONS: Length: 4.46m (176in); **width:** 1.70m (67in); **height:** 1.47m (58in); **wheelbase:** 2.53m (99in); **track:** front 1.47m (58in), rear 1.46m (57in).

KERB WEIGHT: 1442kg (3179lb).

CAPACITIES: Fuel: 60 litres (13.2gal); **boot:** 356 litres (12.6ft^3), 1266 litres (44.7ft^3) with rear seats folded.

PERFORMANCE FIGURES: Top speed: 140mph (225km/h); **0-60mph (96km/h):** 6.1sec; **overall fuel consumption:** 25.2mpg (11.2 litres/100km).

Saab 9-7X

The 9-7X was surely the least Saab-like Saab ever made. Even Bob Lutz reportedly admitted that it was a dilution of the brand, a stopgap solution to tempt customers who were increasingly buying SUVs into Saab's showrooms. It was designed primarily for the North American market, but some cars (all with left-hand drive) were sold in the Middle East and Europe.

The 9-7X was built in Moraine, Ohio on the GMT360 platform, which it shared with the Chevrolet TrailBlazer, Buick Rainier and Oldsmobile Bravada SUVs. It used traditional body-on-frame construction with independent front suspension and a solid axle at the rear, although the suspension was retuned by Saab's engineers in a bid to make it stiffer and more responsive. With the exception of the

The 2005 9-7X seen from the side and rear.

The interior of the 9-7X; all cars had leather upholstery and automatic climate control.

front end, the exterior styling was similar to the Bravada (which was discontinued in 2004).

Inside, the 9-7X had plenty of room for five passengers, and Saab included some characteristic design cues, such as joystick controls for the air vents and green instrument lighting. Ultimately, however, even *Car and Driver* magazine called it "An unconvincing and overpriced badge job of the Chevy TrailBlazer."

Two all-American powerplants were available when the 9-7X went on sale at the start of 2005: a 4.2-litre in-line six developing 275bhp (SAE), and a 5.3-litre 'small-block' V8 producing 300bhp (SAE). All cars had four-wheel drive and used GM's familiar four-speed automatic transmission.

In 2005, two trim levels were offered: Linear and Arc, mirroring the names Saab used on its other models. These were renamed for 2006 as the 4.2i and 5.3i respectively. For the 2008 model year, Saab added a new Aero version at the top of the range, with no less an engine than the 6.0-litre LS2 V8 used in the Chevrolet Corvette: this delivered 390bhp (SAE) and a massive 542Nm (400lb·ft) of torque. The 5.3-litre V8 gained a 'Displacement on Demand' (cylinder cut-off) function to reduce fuel consumption.

GM closed its plant at Moraine in December 2008, bringing production of the 9-7X to an end, with the last cars sold during 2009.

9-7X 5.3i

NUMBER PRODUCED: 20,417 (all models).
PRICE (US – 2006): $41,240.
ENGINE: Longitudinally mounted 90-degree V8 petrol with two valves per cylinder, aluminium alloy cylinder head and block, water-cooled, sequential fuel-injection. Three-way catalytic converter and Lambda sensor. **Bore:** 96mm; **stroke:** 92mm; **capacity:** 5328cc. **Compression ratio:** 9.9:1; **maximum power:** 300bhp (SAE) at 5200rpm; **maximum torque:** 447Nm (330lb·ft) at 4000rpm.

The 5.3-litre Vortec V8.

Memories of happier times? A 9-7X towing a 96 from 1960.

TRANSMISSION: Four-speed Hydra-Matic automatic transmission with floor change. Electronically controlled limited-slip differential. **Final drive ratio:** 3.73:1.
BRAKES: Ventilated discs at front and rear. ABS and ESP.
WHEELS & TYRES: 18in wheels, 255/55 R 18 Dunlop Sport tyres.
SUSPENSION: Front: independent, with double wishbones and coil springs; **rear:** five-link solid axle with electronically controlled air suspension. Bilstein shock absorbers and anti-roll bars at front and rear.
STEERING: Rack and pinion with hydraulic power assistance; **turning circle:** 11.1m (36ft).
DIMENSIONS: Length: 4.91m (193in); **width:** 1.92m (76in); **height:** 1.74m (69in); **wheelbase:** 2.87m (113in); **track:** front 1.60m (63in), rear 1.58m (62in).
KERB WEIGHT: 2169kg (4782lb).
CAPACITIES: Fuel: 83 litres (18.3gal); **boot:** 1127 litres (39.8ft^3), 2268 litres (80.1ft^3) with rear seats folded. **Maximum towing weight:** 2948kg (6500lb).
PERFORMANCE FIGURES: Top speed (limited): 120mph (193km/h); **0-60mph (96km/h):** 7.3sec; **overall fuel consumption:** 18mpg (16 litres/100km).

Saab 9-4X

Following the 9-2X, Saab originally planned to produce a mid-sized crossover based on the Subaru Tribeca, to be known as the 9-6X. In 2005, however, GM sold its stake in Subaru's parent company, Fuji Heavy Industries, and the project was cancelled. GM started work instead on the 9-4X as a replacement for the bigger 9-7X, production of which came to an end in December 2008.

The 9-4X was based on the second-generation Cadillac SRX, built on the GM Theta Premium platform. It was a more modern and compact design than the 9-7X and looked quite different from the sharp-edged Cadillac, with a cleaner, more European design. The interior was similar to the 9-5 NG, with the same dashboard featuring three deeply cowled dials with green backlighting and an advanced infotainment system.

The 9-4X concept shown at the 2008 Detroit Auto Show used Saab's 2.0 Turbo BioPower engine, but for production two V6 petrol engines were offered: a naturally aspirated 3.0-litre unit producing 265bhp (SAE), available with front- or all-wheel drive, and a twin-turbo 2.8-litre developing 300bhp (SAE) for the range-topping Aero model. Saab

The second-generation Cadillac SRX made its debut in 2009.

Front and rear three-quarter views of the production 9-4X.

The dashboard of the 9-4X Aero.

intended to offer diesel engines as well, which would undoubtedly have helped its sales in Europe, but these plans never came to fruition.

Both versions had a six-speed automatic transmission. XWD (four-wheel drive) models had the eLSD electronic limited-slip differential and torque vectoring that Saab had introduced on the 9-3 Turbo X. This could be combined with Saab's new 'DriveSense' adaptive chassis technology, which modified the damping, steering assistance and throttle and gearbox

From its presentation at the Los Angeles Auto Show in November 2010, the career of the 9-4X lasted just 12 months.

mapping via three preset modes: Intelligent, Sport and Comfort.

Production of the 9-4X began at GM's Ramos Arizpe plant in Mexico in February 2011 and it went on sale in June. Unfortunately, fewer than 1000 cars were built (all of them with left-hand drive) before Saab filed for bankruptcy and production ended in November that year.

9-4X Aero XWD Turbo 6

NUMBER PRODUCED: 733 (all models).
PRICE (US): $48,835.
ENGINE: Transversely mounted 60-degree V6 petrol, aluminium alloy cylinder head and block, four overhead camshafts (two per bank), four valves per cylinder with variable valve timing. Bosch Motronic 9.6 engine management with sequential fuel-injection and twin-scroll Mitsubishi turbocharger with intercooler, running 0.8bar (11.6psi) boost. **Bore:** 89mm; **stroke:** 74.8mm; **capacity:** 2792cc. **Compression ratio:** 9.5:1; **maximum power:** 300bhp (SAE) at 5500rpm; **maximum torque:** 400Nm (295lb·ft) at 2000-5000rpm.
TRANSMISSION: Six-speed Aisin-Warner automatic transmission with manual mode via paddle shifters. **Final drive ratio:** 3.75:1.
BRAKES: Ventilated discs at front and rear, dual circuit with vacuum booster. ABS, TCS and ESP standard.
WHEELS & TYRES: 8J x 20in, 235/55 R 20 tyres.
SUSPENSION: Front: MacPherson struts with aluminium lower control arm, coil springs, hydraulic shock absorbers and anti-roll bar; **rear:** independent, linked H-arm layout with coil springs, gas-filled shock absorbers and hollow-section anti-roll bar.
STEERING: Rack and pinion with speed-sensitive power assistance; **turning circle:** 11.9m (39ft).
DIMENSIONS: Length: 4.83m (190in); **width:** 1.91m (75in); **height:** 1.48m (58in); **wheelbase:** 2.81m (111in); **track (front & rear):** 1.62m (64in).
KERB WEIGHT: 2085kg (4597lb).
CAPACITIES: Fuel: 80 litres (17.6gal); **boot:** 485 litres (17.1ft^3) with rear seats up. Maximum towing weight: 2000kg (4409lb).
PERFORMANCE FIGURES: Top speed: 143mph (230km/h); **0-62mph 100km/h):** 8.3sec; **overall fuel consumption:** 23mpg (12 litres/100km).

Also by Julian Parish

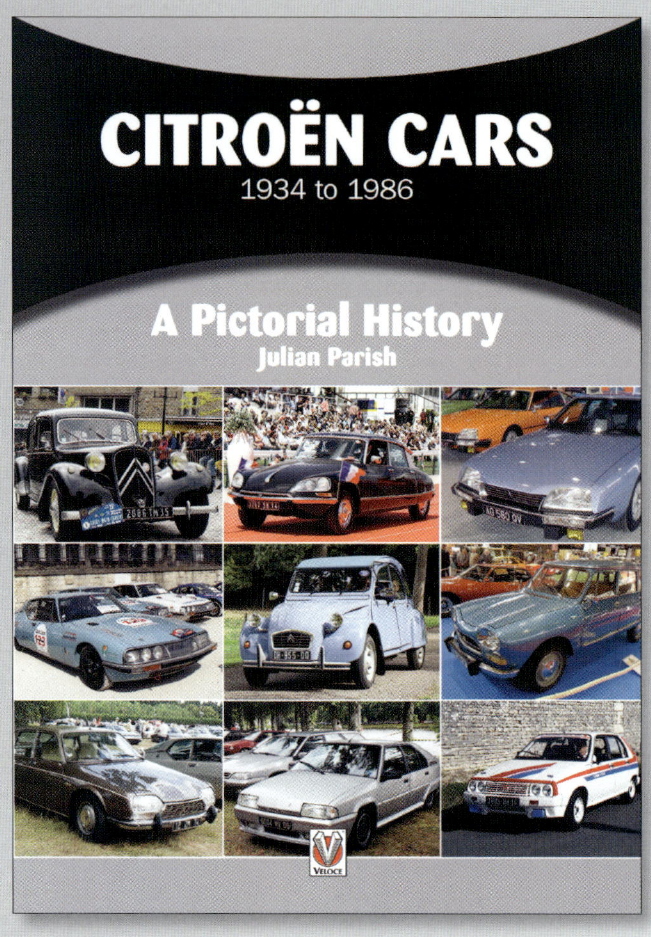

Covers all Citroën's key models from the 1930s to the 1980s, including the Traction Avant, 2CV and DS. Background information on the design of the cars, detailed technical specifications and production data are provided for each model, all extensively illustrated with full-colour photographs and informative diagrams.

ISBN: 9781836440321

Available from all good booksellers or at www.veloce.co.uk

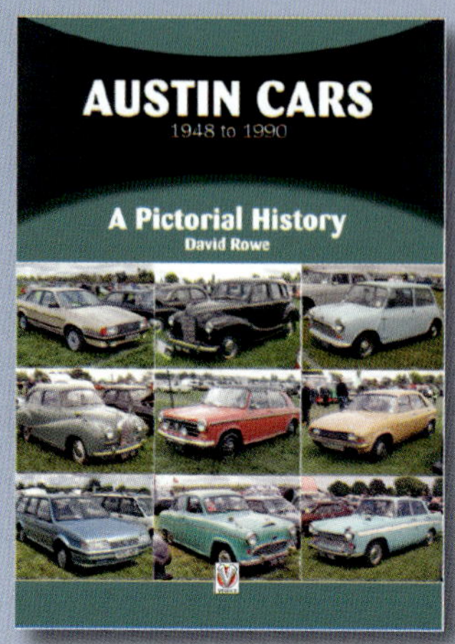

ISBN: 978-1-787112-19-3
• 112 pages • 275 pictures

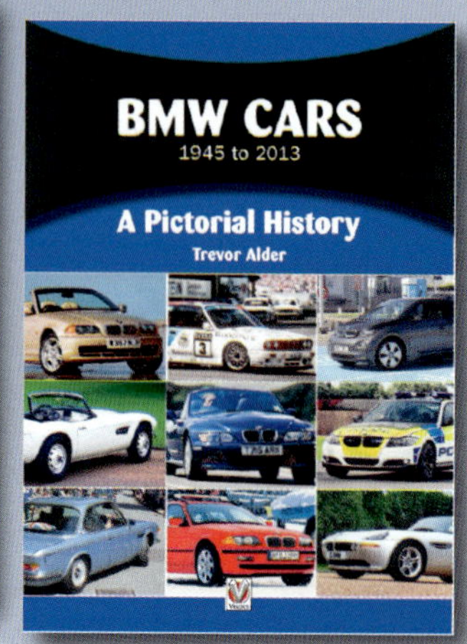

ISBN: 978-1-836440-03-1
• 160 pages • 350 pictures

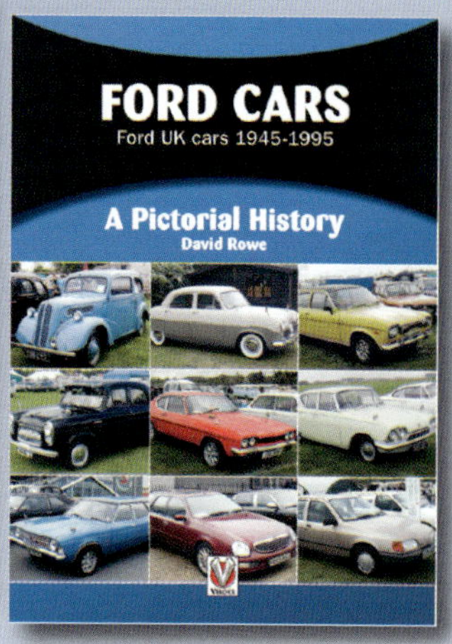

ISBN: 978-1-787116-42-9
• 160 pages • 330 pictures

A Pictorial History – the series

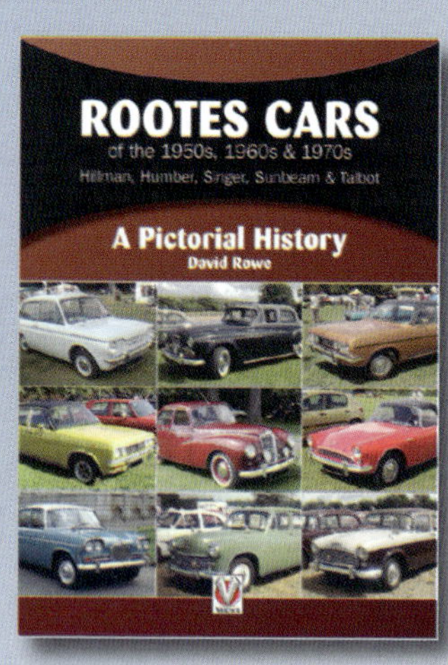

ISBN: 978-1-787114-43-2
• 168 pages • 1083 pictures

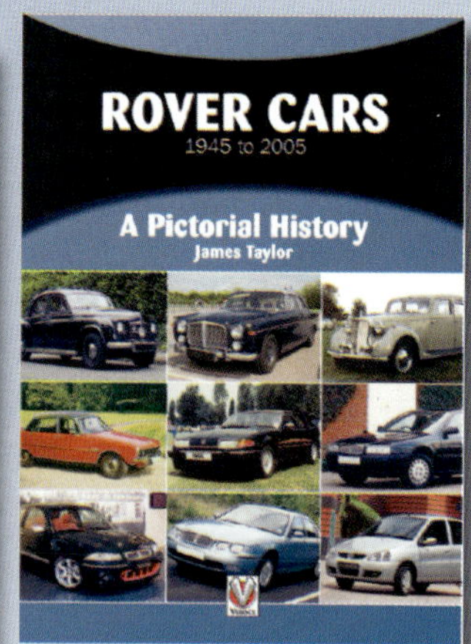

ISBN: 978-1-787116-09-2
• 80 pages • 300 pictures

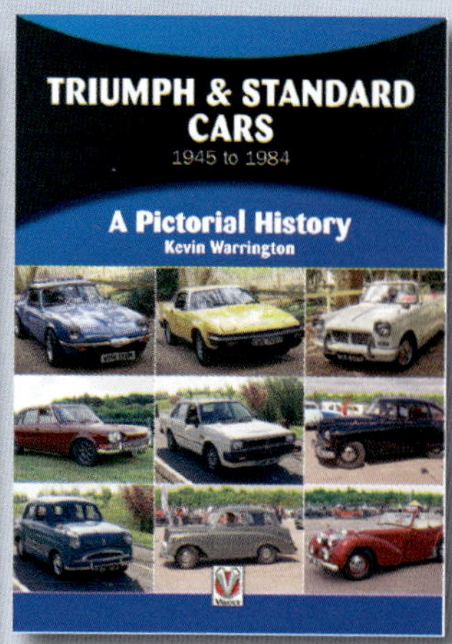

ISBN: 978-1-787110-77-9
• 96 pages • 244 pictures

INDEX